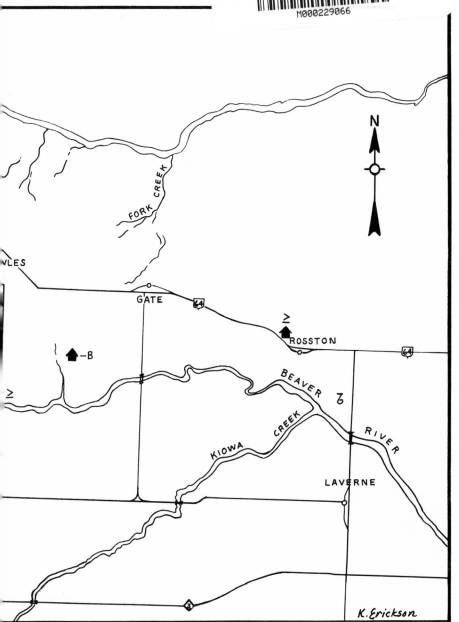

N

FORK CREEK

VLES

GATE 64

ROSSTON 64

B

BEAVER River

KIOWA CREEK

LAVERNE

K. Erickson

Cowboy Country

Cowboy Country

by

John R. Erickson

Photography by

Kristine Erickson

Maverick Books

Other Books by John R. Erickson

Through Time and the Valley (1978)
Panhandle Cowboy (1980)
The Modern Cowboy (1981)
The Devil in Texas (1982)
Hank the Cowdog (1983)
Cowboys Are Partly Human (1983)
The Further Adventures of Hank the Cowdog (1983)
Alkali County Tales (1984)
Hank the Cowdog: It's a Dog's Life (1984)
Ace Reid: Cowpoke (1984)
The Hunter (1984)
Hank the Cowdog and Murder in the Middle Pasture (1985)
Hank the Cowdog: Faded Love (1985)
Essays on Writing & Publishing (1985)
Hank the Cowdog: Let Sleeping Dogs Lie (1986)
Cowboys Are a Separate Species (1986)
Hank the Cowdog & The Curse of the Incredible, Priceless Corncob (1986)
Cowboy Country (1986)

Parts of this book were first published in *Western Horseman, The Cattleman, Farm and Ranch Living,* and *Livestock Weekly.*

International Standard Book Number: 0-916941-17-5

Library of Congress Catalog Card Number: 86-61682

Maverick Books
Box 549
Perryton, Texas 79070
806–435–7611

This book is dedicated to the cowboys everywhere, but especially to the men I worked with on the Beaver River.

Contents

Illustrations

Introduction

It was eight years ago that I rode with the cowboys described in this book. Since that time a small industry has grown up in United States, devoted to the proposition that the cowboy is a vanishing breed and a dying species.

Nobody has ever died more times or jerked more tears than the American cowboy. If this keeps up much longer, he's liable to be spending more time posing for photographs than working stock. Instead of vanishing, he's going to become a professional dier.

I can't help remembering what old Charlie Russell wrote to a friend, back around 1910 as I recall: "The West is dead, my friend."

Russell was a shrewd man with a cowboy's eye for small details. He saw the passing of cowboying as he had known it, and no doubt he was right in the specifics. Charlie's West, the one he had known and loved as a young man, had passed into memory, crowded out by railroads and fences and native sod broken out into farmland.

But in the wider sense, he was wrong. The West wasn't dead, and it still isn't dead. The cowboy may be a vanishing breed, but he's harder to put out of business than a cockroach. Every time we get him laid out in a casket, the rascal kicks the lid open and climbs out again.

Yes, things change. There's no stopping that. But the cowboy has proved himself pretty adaptable, like the old coyote. They thought at one time the coyote was a vanishing breed too, that the sprawl of suburbia would push him into oblivion, but instead of becoming extinct, he learned to open garbage cans and eat poodles.

The cowboy is holding his own too, in spite of the obituaries. His range is shrinking in most places. The pastures are being cut up into smaller units and fenced off, as ranchers experiment with rotational grazing concepts and search for ways of lowering their cost of labor (which means looking for ways of doing without cowboys). The brush is being cleared and the wild brushy cattle replaced with higher-bred bovines that promise better weaning weights and a more docile temperament.

Many ranches that used to run herd bulls on commercial cows are now going to artificial insemination and embryo transplants, which offer maximum use of good bloodlines without the expense of maintaining the actual animals.

I'm glad I missed out on that. When I was cowboying, there were certain things I wouldn't have done. Trading in my horse for a motorcycle was one. Working for an outfit that didn't allow roping was another. And doing the job God intended for a bull to do was another.

I figure that if the cowboy can survive the indignity of breeding his own cows by hand and milking sperm out of a fat lazy bull, he will have adapted to the very worst the modern age has to offer.

No ranch I ever worked for got involved with artificial insemination. If it had, I would have joined old Russell in saying, "The West is dead, my friend," gone to town and got a job as a welder or truck driver.

But some young fellow would have been there to take my place. That's the way it's always been. Just as one generation of cowboys quits in disgust, another moves in and keeps the profession alive.

What's interesting about all this is that the same society that is putting pressure on the cowboy from all directions has an insatiable appetite for art and rituals that depict the *old ways*. Western art and sculpture, which have enjoyed such a tremendous boom in recent years, celebrate the old virtues of courage, independence, and pride of the individual. I have never seen a piece of western art that showed an AI technician at work in a sterile environment, have you? Or a guy out riding the range on his Honda three-wheeler?

So while we're pushing the old-time cowboy out of our life with one hand, we're re-creating him with the other, through art and sculpture — and also, I would say, in roping contests and cutting-horse competitions.

Which raises a question: if we really love the old ways so much, why don't we try to keep them around *in life* instead of in art and rituals?

Many an hour when I've been out prowling pastures, I've puzzled over that question, and I never came up with an answer. Perhaps there's a need in us to destroy what we know to be good and pure, because measuring up to an ideal is too much trouble.

Yet we don't want to live without it either, so we rebuild it in a different form. A cowboy in bronze is okay because we can respond to it with nostalgia and longing. But a cowboy in the flesh reminds us of our own shortcomings, that we don't want to pay the price he has paid for his bit of glory—the hands and feet numb with cold, the broken bones, the fear, the loneliness, the poverty, the aching back, the blood and sweat.

Or maybe the answer lies not so much in the human heart as in strict economics. Our economy has a way of feeding on the past. Yesterday's forest becomes today's coal-generated electricity. Yesterday's mountain becomes today's steel industry. Yesterdays ranches become today's suburbs.

We're a people in a hurry. We consume things quickly. When something gets in our way, we remove it.

Maybe the old cowboy is getting in our way. He never was much of a money-maker. He was too slow, too wedded to the past, too romantic and stubborn and independent. At one time we needed him, but now we don't. Economic realities have changed.

And so the cowboy, once a workingman who did a job, is being changed and consumed. In our time and before our eyes, we are in the process of converting him and his simple values into new forms he never dreamed of: rodeo, country music, cigarette ads, beer commercials, art, sculpture, books, magazines, calendars, western wear, museums, street names, and even the name of America's favorite football team.

Is the cowboy a vanishing breed? Will we wake up one day and find that the flesh-and-blood man has gone and left us with nothing but his mythic presence? I hate to admit that could happen, yet I suppose that deep down, I share Russell's fear that eventually our pell-mell way of life will do the cowboy in—or at least tame him so much that he won't be worthy of the name.

And I guess that's what this book is all about. As a young writer, I had the opportunity to sample the cowboy life, with all its rigors and hardships. It wasn't an easy thing to do, either for me or for my family, but we believed it was the right course.

I cowboyed full-time for almost eight years and worked on ranches in the Texas and Oklahoma Panhandles. These stories come from my experiences on the Beaver River in 1978 and 1979. By that time, I had published one book and a number of articles, and I knew that writing was my calling.

But I was also aware that a writer should be able to do more than string words together. The first requirement of good writing, it seemed to me, was that the writer have something to say. If you are called to be a storyteller, then you must go out and find the stories to tell. I chose to gather stories from experience, rather than from books, and to draw my material from a breed of men I deeply admired—cowboys.

It was my belief then—and it remains so today—that anyone who writes honestly and well about the American cowboy will always find an audience, because whether or not he rides with us into the next century, the cowboy will always be with us as a spiritual force.

He's in our blood and bones. He's so much a part of what we are as a people that we couldn't get rid of him if we wanted to. To know the cowboy is to understand what is good and decent and hopeful in the American experience.

And that's what these stories are about: the men I worked with in Cowboy Country—the real ones, the ones who paid the price.

The author, John Erickson.

Dreaming the dream.

Chapter 1

The Dream

I think every cowboy has a dream of moving on to a country that's bigger and wilder than what he's known before, where the fences and windmills are farther apart, where the horses are a little ranker, where the cowboy crews are bigger, where a man can climb on his horse in the morning and ride all day without seeing or hearing another human being.

There are certain names and places that evoke that dream, places a guy has heard about or read about: Montana, northeastern New Mexico, the Davis Mountains of far west Texas, the Canadian River country in the Texas Panhandle. Now and then you run into a man who's worked those big pastures and big herds, you hear his stories and you think, "That's where the *real* cowboys are, and some day . . . some day I'm going to pack up and move out there, ride with the best and find out what I'm made of."

Maybe that's an odd dream for a young man to have in the age of computers and space travel and cement cities. It's an old-fashioned kind of dream, the kind our great-grandfathers had back in the 1880s as they left the comforts of Ohio and Kentucky and Missouri and plunged into the vastness of the West.

Louis L'Amour understands that tug on a man's heart, and so does every old boy I ever met who has cowboy blood in his veins. I've dreamed that dream too.

It used to hit me at certain times of the year—in the spring when I got the first whiff of green grass; in August when the wind died and the windmills didn't pump and the days were so still that you could hear all the way into next week; in October when the first northers blew in and a crisp wind rattled the cottonwood leaves and whispered in the dried grass.

At those times, my eyes went to the horizons and my mind flew to distant mountains and rivers, where the *real* cowboys gathered at first light and rode out to do their work.

In April of 1978 I was taking care of a 5,000 acre ranch in the Oklahoma Panhandle. It was a cow-calf operation located in the

high sandhills north of the Beaver River. I'd been there for four
years and it had been a good learning ranch for me. I'd had plenty of
adventures, which I later wrote about in the book *Panhandle Cowboy*, and I could have stayed there the rest of my life.

Oh, I still had those cowboy dreams of moving on, but we were
comfortable on the Crown Ranch. I worked for people who left me
alone and treated me right. We lived in a nice house and I had a wife
and two little kids.

If you're young and single, you can sack up your saddle and
move on, but when the kids come along, all at once you have toys
and clothes and diaper bags and baby bottles and play pens.

For most of us, the cowboy dream never really dies. It slowly
fades away and loses its urgency until, around the age of 35 or 40, a
guy finds himself satisfied with where he is or thinking about a job
in town that will pay better money. When he gets a little age on him,
he's not so quick to uproot his family and drag them off to a wilder
place.

A lot of cowboy dreams have ended there. Maybe the wife
says no. Maybe the man wants to spare his kids that long school-bus
ride into town every day. Or maybe he doesn't have the stomach to
pack up all the danged toys and plates and stuff.

I was 35 in April of 1978 when my boss drove out to the ranch
and we sat down in the living room and had a beer. We talked about
the grass and the cattle, and then he said, "John, we're going to put
the ranch up for sale. You'd better start looking around for another
job."

I was a little bitter at first. I'd come to think of that ranch as
mine. I'd ridden horseback over every square foot of those sandhills, and I'd had my nose buried in several of them by a big
Thoroughbred mare named Gypsy. I'd thought I was tougher than
she was, but she'd sort of straightened me out on that.

I'd given that ranch four good years. I'd given it blood and
sweat. I'd just about decided to stay there until they hauled me out
in a box.

The bitter feelings passed pretty quickly. It wasn't my ranch,
never had been. Nobody had ever promised me a lifetime job. My
boss had been good to me, I'd had some fine old times, I'd made him
a good hand, and now it was over.

After the anger came fear. In thirty days I would lose my job,
my home, my salary, my security. It's one thing to have that
cowboy dream when you've got a paycheck coming in every
month. It's a little different, though, when you look it square in the

eyes. Then you begin to wonder. You become aware of your weak spots and your age: you ain't a bronc stomper, you ain't the best roper around, and you ain't even the second-best roper around. Maybe you ain't all the cowboy you've thought you were, and maybe it's time for you to take a pumper's job and move to town. If a pumper's job had popped up right then, I might have taken it. It would have been the easy thing to do. Pumpers worked regular hours, made good money, got all sorts of benefits, and they didn't have to worry about sour horses or busted legs or getting a finger caught in the dallies.

But around the middle of April, one of my cowboy friends came by the ranch. His wife had left him six months before and he'd taken a job down on the Beaver River, on the headquarters place of the old Otto Barby ranch. He'd been living out there alone, thirty miles from the nearest town.

That was real cowboy country down there and he loved the work, but he was lonely and tired of eating cold beans out of a can. He wanted to find another wife and start over again, and he was definitely in the wrong place for that.

"I heard you were looking for a job," he said, "and I thought you might want to know that I'm leaving the first of May."

Well, that sent a little thrill through my bones. In our part of the world, when you talked about Real Cowboys you were talking about the boys down on the river, and never mind about Montana and the Davis Mountains. The work down on the river got about as western as you'd want it to be, and those boys could handle anything that came along. I'd met some of them and knew others by reputation.

They were the best.

A guy dreams of working with the best, but in practice it involves some risks. When you work by yourself on a one-man outfit, you're the top hand and you can talk yourself into a lot of vanity. But go out and ride with the best and you're playing a game with a new set of rules. The ante goes up. You start at the bottom and have to prove yourself to a class of men who aren't easily impressed. It's hard enough to do that when you're 18 and still a little crazy, but when you're 35, it's harder still.

All at once the dream of going to bigger country and a tougher life was within my reach, and when I wasn't giddy with excitement, I was scared out of my wits. There was only one thing that scared me worse: not having a job in May.

So one Sunday afternoon I drove down to the river, about

fifteen miles from the Crown Ranch, and talked to John and May Little about the job.

May's father, Otto Barby, had come to this country in the 1880s, before Oklahoma was a state. He'd worked for an outfit called the Comanche Pool which headquartered in Coldwater, Kansas, and ran 150,000 head of stock. In 1894 he'd gone to work for the Fred Tainter ranch, headquartered on a tributary of the Cimarron River, due north of what is now Knowles, Oklahoma. In '86 he married May Beebe and the couple moved into a dugout near the Beaver River. Starting out with 160 acres, Mr. Barby spent his life acquiring land and improving his holdings, and when he died in 1956 at the age of 90, he had put together 80,000 acres of fine country along the Beaver River, one of the biggest ranches in Oklahoma.

Two years after his death, he was entered into the Cowboy Hall of Fame, and in 1974 *The Record-Stockman* named him one of the Stockmen of the Century.

On his death, the original ranch was divided up among his heirs. In 1978 there were six Barby ranches along the river, and although they operated as separate entities, they were linked by blood and tradition.

To work for one Barby ranch was to work for them all. A man had his home ranch to look after, but when the neighbors needed help, he dropped what he was doing and helped the neighbors. During the busy seasons—spring branding and fall shipping—all the cowboys worked together in one big crew that started at one end of the Barby country and went all the way to the other.

Roundup seasons lasted weeks, not days, and if a man loved cowboying, this was the place to be.

I got the job on the LD Bar, and the first week in May found us moving our things in a stock trailer, over fifteen miles of roads that were either dusty or muddy, depending on what the weather had done that day. On the 8th of May, around six o'clock in the afternoon, I pulled in with the last load, which included our two dogs and a two-year old mare that I was in the process of breaking.

I turned the mare out into the horse trap and was ready to go to the house, when Mr. Little came down to the barn and told me that Ralph Barby's Open A ranch had called and they wanted me to be at Rosston the next morning at daylight. The crew was going to round up a nine section pasture.

"Where is Rosston?" I asked. I'd been on the ranch just long

The Erickson family on the John Little Ranch, 1978: Kris, John, Scot (4), and Ashley (1).

enough to find my way from the house to the barn and that was about it.

"It's thirty miles northeast of here."

I did some quick calculating. To be there at daylight with a saddled horse and trailer, I would have to get up around four in the morning. If I didn't get lost on unfamiliar winding roads, I could make it.

But one small problem remained: my mare was too young for a hard day's work and I hadn't seen any other horses in the trap. "What am I going to ride?"

Mr. Little said I would have four horses in my string, but they were all out on the river. Clever brutes, they had figured out how to jump the cattle guard and get to the good tender grass down in the meadow.

I checked the sun. We had about thirty minutes of daylight and then maybe thirty minutes of twilight. If Mr. Little's horses co-operated, we might get a saddlehorse in the corral before dark. If they didn't cooperate, if they sensed that we were desperate and in a hurry, they would probably go bucking off into the tamaracks, laughing all the way and leaving me afoot.

I had been in that position many times before and I had never learned to like it.

I got a bucket of feed and a bridle, and we drove down to the river. I could see them along the west fence, two sorrels, a bay, and a squatty dun mare.

"Which one should I ride?"

"The one you can catch."

Their ears went up and they watched us. Little John, the bay, must have smelled a rat because he started slinking way—glancing back, studying our movements, determining our purpose. Then he tossed his head, kicked up his heels, and galloped into the brush.

He knew why we were there, and he knew just exactly how to make us look and feel like a couple of monkeys.

Ginger, the sorrel mare, went with him to the river, but Star and the dun mare stayed on the fence. We stopped about fifty feet from them and I got out with the feed bucket. Lucky for me, Star was a big friendly 1300 pound pup, the kind that wouldn't cheat you or leave you afoot without a pretty good reason. And Honey, the dun, had a nice disposition too.

They came over and sampled the feed. I let them have a few bites, then I reached my arm around Star's neck.

The old rascal could have run off and dragged me all over that ranch if he'd wanted to, but he didn't. I slipped off my belt and put it around his neck, reached into the Bronco for the bridle, and put it on.

The sun had gone down and the river country was slipping into deep purple shadows. We hadn't brought a saddle, so my first ride on this horse would have to be bareback, in half-darkness.

We loped back to headquarters. I hated to lope a strange horse when I didn't have a horn to hang to, but I didn't want to spend all night trying to find my way home either. If old Star had had any meanness in him, he could have bedded me down without much trouble, but he didn't.

I left him up for the night, grained him good, and then made preparations for the next day — put gas in the pickup, hitched up the stock trailer, and laid out my chaps, saddle, spurs, and rope where I could find them the next morning at 4:30.

My first full day as a Beaver River cowboy was going to start early, and it was likely to be a long one.

John Erickson and Honey, ready for work.

Chapter 2

The Big Roundup

The next morning at daylight I approached the shipping pens, about two miles west of Rosston. I could see ten or twelve pickup-trailer rigs parked out front. When I pulled off the highway, there were two rigs behind me and another one or two coming in from the east, headlights still glowing.

My headlights cut across a group of cowboys, more than a dozen of them, wearing leather vests and denim jackets against the morning chill. They stood around talking. Some had brought thermoses of hot coffee and they passed them around to the other men. Some were zipping up their shotgun chaps, others buckled on their spurs, others led their horses out of trailers.

This roundup had pulled in cowboys from an area fifty miles in all directions. Most of them worked on ranches along the Beaver River, from Beaver City to Laverne, a distance of forty miles. But others had come from ranches on Kiowa Creek, the Cimarron River, and even Crooked Creek up in Meade County, Kansas.

They had all come to take part in rounding up one of the biggest pastures in the Oklahoma Panhandle. I had heard stories about the Rosston river pasture. It consisted of 6,000 acres under one fence, and it was rough and hard to gather. The northern three-quarters of the pasture was composed of high, brushy sand-hills. Finding cattle in the hills was difficult, and riding a horse up and down, through loose footing, wore him down in a hurry.

But the southern quarter of the pasture was even worse. Along the flood plain of the Beaver River, the crew faced a jungle of tamarack brush, about three miles long and a mile wide. In the middle of this maze you could lose your sense of direction. You had to pick your way through trails made by deer and cattle, while avoiding slews that could bog a horse and river crossings that might turn out to be quicksand.

I had heard that the cattle in this pasture were wild and "brushy," and that they often had to be roped and dragged out of the tamaracks. I had heard about the time this pasture was rounded up in a heavy fog and cowboys had gotten lost and stayed lost for hours. I had heard about horses going down in quicksand and about cowboys meeting low branches in the midst of a chase.

I had heard about the time Joe Martin rode a green mare on this roundup. The mare bucked him off out in the tamaracks and broke his nose. Hours away from a doctor or a hospital, he straightened his nose and finished the roundup.

For years I'd wanted to work this roundup, and at last, here I was.

But I was a little uneasy about it. For one thing, I would be mounted on a horse I had never ridden before. I knew old Star had good size, but I didn't know about his speed, quickness, endurance, or if he was sure-footed.

And I was also concerned about my roping. I knew these river outfits used the rope a lot, and they were good. Every year at the Beaver Rodeo, you'd see five or six river cowboys in the roping events.

I considered myself an average roper, your ordinary three-loop cowboy who, given enough time, could put the noose where it was supposed to go and get the job done. On the Crown Ranch, that had gotten me by. But I had an idea that down here on the river, that wouldn't be good enough.

I pulled up to the shipping pens and got out, found Darrell Cox, the Open A foreman, and introduced myself as the new hired man on Uncle John Little's ranch. Darrell was a man of medium height and build. He had a kind face and a gentle smile. He wore glasses and an old felt hat, and he had a pinch of snuff inside his lower lip. He was cordial and welcomed me to the crew, but after a short conversation, he had to go on about his business.

I stood alone, feeling like the new kid on the block. The other men didn't come up and introduce themselves. Cowboys aren't particularly good mixers, and they don't go out of their way to observe social amenities. They're more likely to stay away from a new man and watch him—the way he handles his horse, how he conducts himself, how much he talks, and how well he handles his territory.

If he makes a hand and tends to his business, the older guys will come around after a week or so and introduce themselves. But they do it at their own pace, and there's no way you can speed up the process.

The pickups and trailers kept pulling in, and the crew swelled to twenty-three men. At last I saw a familiar face in the crowd, and I went over and said hello to Alfred Barby.

Alfred and his brother Rusty Barby owned the 76 Ranch, a 36,000 acre cow-calf operation that was spread out in two counties in Kansas and two counties in Oklahoma. They were second cousins of the Barbys on the Beaver River, and Alfred swapped out roundup work with Darrell Cox's outfit every spring and fall.

I had met Alfred a few months before, when I had written an article about a herd of buffalo he kept on his ranch north of Laverne, Oklahoma. He had told me that buffalo have to be handled in a special way, that they don't behave the same as cattle.

You don't ride into the herd and try to cut out a single animal, as you might do with cattle. Buffalo have a powerful herd instinct and won't allow themselves to be split up. And you don't want to put yourself between a cow and her calf, since buffalo are pretty serious about motherhood.

If cornered and provoked, buffalo can be dangerous. Alfred said they are exceptionally quick, and where cattle might try to go around you, a buffalo will run over you. Working pens must be tall and stout to hold them, and they must be hauled in covered trailers or else they will jump out.

Alfred pointed out that the buffalo have certain characteristics that make them attractive as commercial meat animals: natural resistance to disease and insects, no calving problems, survival instincts, and a lifespan of 20 to 30 years (Charles Goodnight, the Texas rancher who probably saved the species from extinction, claimed that one of his buffalo cows bred back at the age of 35.) The meat is very lean and tastes a good deal like beef.

But they have some disadvantages too, the main one being temperament. In captivity, buffalo gentle down but never entirely lose their wild instincts, which means that to keep the brutes around, you need to have a taste for cowboying in the rough.

I had gotten the feeling that Alfred Barby was that kind of man. He certainly looked the part. He must have been in his early sixties when I first met him, yet he had the physique and rugged good looks of a man half his age. He looked as good ahorseback as any man I'd ever seen: a big, stout, proud-looking man who seemed to have been made for cowboy clothes.

Anyway, I was glad to see him at the roundup. I walked over and shook his big hand, and he introduced me to his son Bill. We chatted until seven o'clock. The sun was up by then, and Darrell

Cox appeared and told us to load our horses into four or five
trailers. I loaded old Star into Alfred's rig and rode to the jump-
ingoff place with him and Bill.

We drove three or four miles down sandy lease roads, through
the big sage-covered sandhills, until we reached the spot on the west
end of the pasture where Darrell had parked his rig. We unloaded
our horses, tightened our cinches, and mounted up.

Darrell split up the crew, sending half of the riders up into the
sandhills to the north and the other half down into the tamaracks
along the river.

The sun had popped over the horizon, and I looked out at the
country we would be riding through. There was hardly a breath of
wind and the sweet spring air hung still and silent around us. The
country seemed to go on and on without end, the blue-gray hills
rolling down to the river bottom which was still partly shrouded in
a morning haze.

I didn't see a single cow. I had heard someone say that there
were four hundred cows and as many calves in this pasture, yet the
country was so big and rugged that they were invisible.

Alfred rode south toward the river, and since I had attached
myself to him for the day, I went with him. We rode together for a
while and talked. Alfred told me that during the winter he had been
bitten by a coyote, had gotten blood poisoning from the bite, and
had almost lost his hand. He always had good stories to tell and I
loved to hear them, but we soon split up.

Telling stories, talking horses and roping and cattle is one of
the things you love to do at a roundup. It just seems a natural thing
to do when your belly is still warm with coffee and the sun is
beginning to burn some of the chill out of the air and you're rocking
along in time with your horse. But you're there on business, and you
don't want one of your cowboy friends to look over in your direction
and grumble, "Huh! Two men riding one horse."

Alfred and I had been assigned an area to cover, so we split up
and spread out and started hunting cattle. For the next three hours, I
never was within a quarter mile of another man. Now and then I
heard the boys shouting down in the tamaracks and caught a
glimpse of a rider stopped on a sandhill to the north, but that big
pasture pretty well swallowed up 23 cowboys without a trace.

It was just me and old Star, riding out our part of the long line
of cowboys that stretched from one end of the pasture to the other, a
distance of three miles, I would guess. This was slow work and I had
a chance to get a feel for my horse. He hadn't bucked me off in front

of the crew, which I appreciated. That would have been a terrible embarrassment, getting piled my first day on the job.

After we'd ridden for half an hour, I thought I had Star figured out. As I'd suspected the night before, he was just a big old pup that didn't have a malicious bone in his body and probably hadn't even thought about pitching for the last five years. He had some cow sense and he was a willing horse, but he was long on stout and short on speed and endurance. A trip to the top of a sandhill left him huffing and puffing, and I knew I would have to ration out his energy and save something back for the end of the day.

Our line of cowboys rode east across the width of the pasture, until we reached the east fenceline. There, we all turned south and pushed our cattle down into the flat flood plain of the river. When we got there, we had to hold our cattle and wait for the boys on the river to come out of the brush with their stock.

They had gotten the harder part of the job, bringing those brushy cattle out of the shadows and into the light of day. Some of those river cattle had never been gathered before. They were experts at hiding and losing themselves in the brush. They didn't like humans, and they didn't have much use for our roundup.

You could pick out the worst ones at a distance. They came flying out of the tamaracks with their tails curled over their backs in a figure 9 and their heads up in the air. Some were branded cows, but some had never heard of a branding iron. They had grown up in that brush, escaped two roundups a year, and were now teaching their own calves the ways of the wild.

They sure were surprised when they popped out of the brush, took aim for the sandhills, and saw a line of cowboys there on the north side of the river—every man with a rope in his hands and an itch to stick it on a nice set of horns.

We held our line on the north, but some of those old sisters didn't make the trip to the roundup ground. When they saw us blocking their path to the hills, they had the deal figured out. They changed directions and headed back to the brush. Some got stopped and turned around, but others couldn't be stopped with anything but a nylon rope. If you put a horse in their path, they would go under you, over you, or through you, just any way you wanted it.

We spilled some but we got most of them gathered. When all the cowboys came out of the brush, we shaped the herd and started driving them west, up the river, and drove them to a big grassy flat that served as the roundup ground.

We stopped them there and loose-herded them, while Darrell

Cox, Alfred Barby, and Stanley Barby entered the herd and started cutting out dry cows and bulls.

That was something to see—a herd of eight hundred cattle, loose-herded by 23 cowboys. It wouldn't have been uncommon fifty years ago, but these days, in the age of shipping pens and squeeze chutes and ranchers who are too busy to swap out work, it's a pretty rare sight.

I'm glad I got to see it.

Chapter 3

The Branding Pen

On most of the ranches I had worked, cattle were driven to corrals and the cutting and sorting were usually done afoot and through a gate.

The Open A and the other Barby ranches had a different way of doing things. All the sorting was done ahorseback, in the pasture. The cuts were thrown out of the main herd, and one man was sent out to loose-herd them and keep them from wandering away. While the cutters worked inside the herd, the rest of us held them in a big circle.

We had been holding herd for maybe twenty minutes when a three hundred pound calf threw up his head and tail and made a dash for freedom. Several of the boys moved their horses to cut him off, but he went between them and headed for the brush.

A tall, lean young fellow named Shorty Barby (I think there was some irony in his name, since he stood over six feet tall) pulled his black felt hat down to his ears and went after the calf. He caught up with him and tried to turn him back to the herd. The calf dodged past him two or three times and kept running toward the river.

Shorty, who worked for the 76 Ranch at Laverne, took down his rope, built a small loop, and fitted it around the calf's neck on the first toss. Then he stepped off his horse, threw a half-hitch over the calf's nose, and hauled him back to the herd.

Two more calves quit the herd, and they were brought back by other men in the same manner. After that, there was no more bunch-quitting.

It took the cutters about two hours to sort off the dry cows and bulls. Then five cowboys drove the cuts to another pasture, while the rest of us drove the main herd to a branding pen that had been constructed of portable corral panels not far from the roundup ground. There were no permanent corrals in this 6,000 acre pasture, and that turned out to be the case with most of the big pastures along the river.

It was noon by the time we penned the herd, and Jo Ann Cox,

Darrell's wife, had already arrived in her car and started setting up for lunch. We lined up and filled our plates from pots and dishes in the trunk of her car: fried steak, mashed potatoes and gravy, red beans, corn, and big glasses of iced tea. We hunkered on the ground and ate like wolves, then went back for homemade pie.

To feed such a crew of men, Jo Ann must have stayed up half the night cooking, yet she was so calm and pleasant that one got no sense of effort or strain in her manner.

When we had finished, we scraped our plates and put them in a cardboard box in the trunk, then moved to the branding pen and began the main job of the day--branding three hundred and twenty calves.

Several of the boys fired up two propane branding heaters and Darrell assigned the specialized jobs of branding, castrating, and dehorning to the men he wanted. The rest of us paired up into wrestling teams. It would be our job to "rassle" down the calves as they were dragged to the fire by the heelers.

Nobody on the crew was anxious to partner with me, since I was a new man and hadn't proved myself. If a man doesn't know how to handle stock on a rope, his partner has to work twice as hard and runs some risk of injury. A lot of cowboys these days have only worked cattle through a squeeze chute and have never learned the techniques for throwing calves by hand. The chute-method requires very little in the way of brains or skill, but you need both to handle stock on a rope.

No one wants to teach a rookie. I wasn't a rookie, but they didn't know that down on the river.

I stood around for a while and finally partnered up with Bill Barby, Alfred's son. By that time the irons were hot, the vaccine guns were loaded, and the heelers had changed to their rope horses and were easing through the herd.

The success or failure of an old-fashioned branding depends on the quality of the heelers. If they're good, the work moves at a rapid pace. The crew establishes a rhythm and nobody gets tired or hurt. If the heelers aren't so good, the job is much more difficult for everyone.

I have attended a few brandings where the ropers lacked skill and experience. Calves came to the fire roped by the neck and fighting. Branding heaters were knocked over, pails of disinfectant sent splashing, cowboys tripped down by the rope, and nothing worked right. That's the kind of circus that leads old-timers to say, "That rope's just too dangerous. We better go back to the chute."

But a smooth, well-run rope-and-drag branding is a sight to behold--cowboy work raised to poetry. It's not a common sight these days because good heelers aren't very common. Years ago, all the big ranches heeled and dragged, and their heelers were experts at catching in a herd, which is not the same as heeling steers in a roping arena.

An old cowboy once explained to me the difference between heeling in a branding pen and heeling in the arena:

"These kids today have spent all their time in an arena. They go into a branding pen and try to *rope* a calf. Well, the great heelers on the old ranches never *roped* in a branding pen; they *trapped*. They knew how to work their horse and get into the right position, so that when they laid that trap under the calf's belly, he stepped into it every time. They made it look easy, but it took them years and years to learn that."

Our heelers for the day were Stanley Barby, owner of the Bar B Ranch, and one of his cowboys, a fellow named Glenn Green. I knew about Stanley. I'd seen him rope at the Beaver Rodeo and I knew he was considered the best roper in Beaver County, and maybe the entire Oklahoma Panhandle. He could rope calves or either end of a steer in team roping, and he could do it just as well out in the pasture as he could in the arena.

As the old cowboy had pointed out to me, a good arena roper isn't necessarily a good heeler in the branding pen. It's a different style of roping. But Stanley, who was about 40 years old at this time, had mastered herd roping too. I don't know where he picked it up, since his grandfather Barby hadn't allowed much roping on the ranch when Stanley was growing up, but at some point in his life, he must have spent some time studying under an old-time heeler.

He rode into the herd and started pulling out calves faster than we could throw and brand them.

I didn't know Green, the other heeler. He stood about six feet tall and weighed maybe 190 hard pounds. He had broad shoulders and muscular hands. I guessed his age at 45 or 50, though it was hard to tell. He had a lot of grey in his close-cropped hair, but he also had the rugged, weathered good looks of a man in the prime of his life. He had a pair of narrow blue eyes that could either bore a hole right through you or sparkle with mirth and intelligence.

Glenn didn't blend into a crowd. There was something about him that drew your attention. Maybe it was his air of self-confidence, or maybe it was his keen wit. He wasn't one to jabber or make idle talk, but at the noon meal he had made several cracks that

At left, Hobart Hall stands by with a hot iron, while Erickson and Pat Mason (right) take down a calf that Stanley Barby has dragged to the fire.

Branding on the Beaver River. From right, Darrell Cox, Jake Parker, Kary Cox, John Erickson, John Little, and Pat Mason.

sent the whole crew up in gales of laughter. He spoke in a slow drawl, never raised or lowered his voice, and delivered his humor in a dry, folksy manner that cowboys through the years have always admired. When he said something, everyone listened.

I had noticed that the other cowboys showed a great deal of respect to Mr. Green. When the crew went to the water can, Glenn was handed the first cup, even though he usually refused the honor and told the fellow to go ahead and drink. And the younger cowboys, who were always playing pranks on someone, stayed clear of Glenn.

Glenn did his heeling that day on a bay horse named Moose, and the contrast between the dashing Mr. Green and his mount was comical. You didn't need to ask where the horse had gotten his name. In profile, he resembled a dehorned moose.

Glenn, who had learned to rope in the old school, tied his rope hard and fast to the horn (Stanley dallied). And he was a great herd roper.

I watched him for two hours and tried to analyze his heeling style. He slipped through the herd and left the cattle undisturbed. He made no noise and wasted no motion. He could catch from the left side of a calf or from the rear, though it appeared to me that his favorite shot was a throw from the calf's left. He would ease his horse up next to the calf and deliver a small loop over the flank, snapping his wrist at the last moment and placing an open loop right in front of the animal's hind feet.

After throwing the rope, Glenn would turn his horse and ride to the fire without even looking back to see if he had made a catch. Now, that impressed me. Most of us had to watch and fish and manipulate the slack. Not Glenn. Somehow he knew everything was right, that the calf was going to step into the loop.

I watched Glenn and Stanley go through 320 calves in three hours, and I estimated they were both hitting 85-90% of their shots. I doubt that I'll ever see better herd roping.

I've heard old-time cowboys talk about the great herd ropers they knew--men you and I never heard of but whose names were known to all ranch cowboys of their day, men who could heel all afternoon and never miss a shot, men who were the stars and honored guests at every roundup they attended.

I always suspected that maybe those heelers got a little better with each telling of the story, but maybe not. Maybe there actually were men who could heel all afternoon and never miss a shot. I've never met anyone that good, but Stanley and Glenn came pretty close.

After the last calf had been dragged to the fire, Glenn climbed down from old Moose, slacked the cinch, and went over to the water can for a drink. I followed him.

"Glenn, I really enjoyed watching you rope."

He looked at me a moment and smiled. "Thanks."

I had nothing more to say, so I walked away.

Bar B cowboys Pat Mason and Glenn Green. Glenn had gotten into an argument with a bronc several days before and injured his shoulder. No report on the bronc's condition.

Chapter 4

More Spring Roundups

After working several days for Darrell Cox and the Open A outfit, our crew moved up the Beaver River to the Bar B and worked Stanley Barby's river pasture, which was probably four or five sections in size.

My orders for the day were to trailer my horse to the northeast corner of the pasture and to be ready to ride at daylight. Several of the Open A cowboys had been told to start in the southeast corner on the other side of the river, while Stanley and his crew of five would leave from headquarters and work out the river from the west.

The three prongs would meet on the river, near the center of the pasture, and throw the cattle across to the south side and drive them to the roundup ground.

I left home while it was still dark, drove through Leland Barby's Three Cross Ranch, and reached the northeast corner of Stanley's river pasture around ten minutes to seven. Day was just breaking in the east and up ahead, just across the cattle guard, I could see a blue four-wheel drive pickup and a white trailer parked along the side of the road.

I recognized it as Glenn Green's rig. He and I would be working together in the sandhills north of the river.

Glenn wasn't the kind of man who talked much about himself, but I'd picked up a few details here and there. I'd heard that he'd been raised on the Matador Ranch and that he'd left home at an early age and gone to work on a ranch near Santa Rosa, New Mexico, where he rode rough-string horses. This was a big outfit where the crew stayed out with the wagon for months at a time.

He left cowboying during the Korean War and joined the Marines. Out of the service, he returned to Texas and ranch work. He worked for Marshall Cator at Sunray and for Grundy Morrison on the Canadian River. For a while he owned a string of rodeo stock, hauled hay with his own trucks, and then worked as cowboy boss at a feedlot near Hereford.

Glenn had been around and seen a lot of country. He knew, and was known by, just about everyone who had ever cowboyed or rodeoed in the Texas and Oklahoma Panhandles.

There were a few stories about Glenn that were told in whispers—about an only son who had died in a tragic fire, about Glenn's reputation as a fighter. It was hard for me to imagine him as a brawler. In his work, he was stern and precise, yet there was a gentleness about him too, and he had a wonderful sense of humor.

One time he and Moose had some trouble with a wild cow. After a bit of a struggle, they threw her back into the herd and Glenn said to the man next to him, "Imagine her thinking she could get away–her afoot and me ahorseback!"

As a writer, I couldn't help but envy his grasp of irony and his economy of language. Most of us scribblers spend a lifetime learning to write the kind of prose that came out of his mouth without thought or effort.

Anyway, that morning I pulled up beside his rig and we exchanged greetings. Glenn stepped out and pulled on a pair of worn shotgun chaps with a big hole in one knee. He was cordial but kept his distance. He was a man you met through work, not through conversation.

I had brought Little John, and I jumped him out of the stock trailer and took the slack out of my cinches. Glenn unloaded his horse and did the same. He had brought a sorrel horse, one of four or five broncs and half-broncs in his work string.

That was one thing about Glenn Green: you never saw him riding a finished horse. I don't know whether he was breaking horses on the side or if he just found finished horses too dull for his taste, but he could do more on a bronc than most men could do on their favorite old saddlehorse. When he took hold of a horse with those big hands, he could make him do almost anything.

Glenn explained the general roundup strategy to me and we split up. I didn't see him again until we were in the timber down in the river bottom. He was bringing in a bunch of cattle from the east and I had a bunch that I had brought down from the sandhills. We threw them together on the north bank and started pushing them across the river.

I never took my eyes off Glenn. I watched every move he made and put myself in the position to back him up when he gave a lead. He wasn't one to shout orders or explain what he was doing. He expected you to watch and be there.

He was a smooth, efficient horseman. He knew exactly what he was doing all the time and he saw everything that was going on around him. There was no wasted motion when he went to work, and if you watched him and followed his lead, you could be sure that you were doing the job right.

We had to throw about thirty head across the river, which normally ran about a foot deep at this point but was up a bit from recent rains. The cattle sniffed the water and bawled. They didn't want to cross and several of them broke west up the river. We cut them off and turned them back to the crossing.

At last, two cows went into the water. But one bull calf had other ideas. He whirled around and headed north in a run. I spurred Little John and made the proper move to turn him, but I couldn't stop him. He went crashing through the brush and disappeared.

I glanced over at Glenn and waited for him to tell me what to do. Should I go after the calf or stay with the bunch? He said nothing, wasn't even looking at me, and I took that to mean, "Go get him."

I had hoped that Glenn might do the job himself, since he was the roping expert and I was something less than that, but for one reason or another, he chose to give me the job. I didn't know whether this was an honor or a silent rebuke for letting the calf get past me.

I put the spurs to Little John, and off we went after the outlaw.

There was a lot of cottonwood timber in this part of the river bottom, and quite a lot of brush in the form of small willows, grape vines, and wild plum thickets. The calf had vanished into the brush and somehow I had to find him. I rode to the northeast, in the direction he had been running when I had last seen him, and kept my eyes and ears open.

If he stopped and hid himself, I would never find him, and I would have to report back to Glenn that I had failed—a word he probably didn't admire too much. At last I heard something in the brush ahead, rode toward it, and flushed the little scamp out of a plum thicket. I galloped through a clearing and tried to head him back to the river, but he wouldn't turn.

I would either take him back on my nylon or not at all.

I took down my rope, built a loop, and started after him. Little John was hopping over dead logs and I was dodging tree limbs. This wasn't the kind of place you would choose for calf roping. Little John put me into position and I fired. The calf ran through the loop before I could get my slack pulled up. I built another loop and threw again. Another miss.

We were getting farther and farther away from the river cross-ing, and I was feeling the pressure to get the job done and get back to the herd. I hurried my next throw and cursed when it went askew.

Finally I caught him, got behind him, and tried to drive him back to the river. He went perhaps fifty yards and then sulled. I whipped him with the rope but he wouldn't move. I threw a double half-hitch over the saddlehorn, bailed off my horse, flanked the calf down, and did what I had seen Shorty Barby do several days before: I put a "Mexican headstall" on his nose and tried to lead him back to the river. When he wouldn't lead, I dragged him.

I hated to do that because I knew it was hard on cattle, but I couldn't see that I had much of a choice. I either had to drag him or let him go.

I pulled him down to the river, and when he didn't get up, I rode into the water and dragged him across. On the south bank, while he was catching his breath, I stepped down and took off my rope. Glenn came riding out of the timber. He stopped his horse and studied the scene before him.

My horse was breathing hard. The calf was tired. I'm sure Glenn read the signs and knew that I had thrown several loops into the dirt before I'd come up with one that fit.

He didn't say anything, but I got the impression that he wasn't too proud of my work. I had brought the calf back, but it had taken me ten minutes. Glenn would have one-looped him and had him on the south side of the river in two.

It had been a messy job. Glenn didn't say that, but I knew that's what he thought. I coiled up my rope, which was wet and sandy, and tied it back on the horn string.

Once we had pushed the cattle across the river, it was a simple matter to drive them to the roundup ground. Stanley had a nice gentle bunch of cows. They were easy to handle and they respected a horse. Over the years, Stanley had taught them good manners. He didn't tolerate bunch-quitters. On the Bar B, a cow stayed with the herd, by choice or by rope.

I'd heard that at one time in his life, Stanley had used a technique called "tailing" on his bunch-quitters. Instead of roping the beast, you ride up behind her, grab the end of her tail, dally it around the saddlehorn, and then ride off at a sharp angle, spilling her head over heels.

Cowboys out of Old Mexico have used the tailing method for years, but Stanley was the only white man I ever knew who had tried it.

We drove the herd up to the roundup ground, a big flat meadow about half a mile south of the river, and held them while the Open A boys came in from the east with their cattle and Stanley and his Bar B crew came in from the west. When the herd was assembled, Stanley and Pat Mason, one of his cowboys, rode into the bunch and started cutting out the dry cows and bulls.

I never saw a man who was better in a herd than Stanley, even though he was just 40 years old. He could spot a dry cow fifty yards away and have her moving outside the herd before she knew what was going on. He kept his horse in a long walk or a trot all the time. He never made any unneccessary movements or got the cattle stirred up. When he took a cow to the edge of the herd, he already had his next cow spotted.

He worked quickly and quietly, he made very few mistakes, and he was highly predictable. The men outside the herd could watch him and know exactly which cow he was after and where he wanted her to go. If you studied Stanley's techniques in a herd, you could learn just about everything you needed to know on that subject.

After splitting the herd, we drove the cows and calves into a branding trap made of woven wire. Stanley had designed and built it for one purpose: heeling, dragging, and branding. We set up two branding heaters in the middle of the trap and started the roaring propane fires. Stanley heeled and dragged calves from the north end and Pat Mason dragged from the south end. Neither man got in the way of the other, and there was no danger of getting one horse crossed up in the other man's rope.

Pat was a good-sized man, around six feet tall and weighing 190 or 200 pounds. He was big in the arms and shoulders, had a broad friendly face and a strong jaw. He wore a black felt hat with the brim cut down to three inches, probably because the modified version stayed on his head better in the Panhandle wind.

Pat came from a long line of cowboys. His father had ridden rough string horses on the 6666 Ranch, and his uncles and great-uncles had worked all the big ranches down in Texas: the Sixes (6666), the Forks (Pitchfork), the SMS (Swenson), and the JA in Palo Duro Canyon.

And Pat had been around quite a bit himself. I heard him tell about his experiences on the 6666, the Adams Ranch up on the Cimarron, and other ranches in Texas, Oklahoma, and Kansas. He had also told me that he had once held my job on the LD Bar, maybe six or seven years before I arrived there.

Among other things, he had acquired a hatred of Little John, the horse I was riding that day. Pat had once tried to drag a cow into a stock trailer, and Little John had sulled and gotten him into a wreck.

"You watch that horse," he told me. "He'll quit you when you need him the most and get you in trouble."

Pat knew his business, he'd been around, he was smart. He and Glenn Green and Stanley Barby were clearly the best men on the crew. It almost seemed unfair that all three of them worked for the same outfit.

Pat was a lefthanded roper. In 1978 he wasn't as good a heeler as Stanley or Glenn, but he was plenty good and getting better with practice. (The next spring, he and his partner won the team roping at the Beaver Rodeo.)

He used a heeling style that was different from Glenn's. Where Glenn swung his rope above his shoulder and preferred close shots over the hip, Pat swung his loop out to the side and took long shots. Also, where Glenn always tied solid, Pat dallied most of the time, and he was good at it.

As usual, I worked on the ground and wrestled the calves. Some cowboys regard this work as unpleasant or demeaning, and look forward to the day when they can graduate to the "executive" jobs—branding, dehorning, castrating, vaccinating.

I always considered wrestling calves fun and the rest of it work. Any time the boss was looking for a man to run the knife or the dehorning tubes, I ducked my head and tried to hide.

My partner for the day was Carl Githens, an older cowboy who worked for the Open A. He had false teeth, smoked King Edward cigars, and talked all the time. It didn't seem to bother him that I was the new man on the crew, and we worked well together.

We went through three hundred calves in just a few hours. We worked up a sweat, but nobody got hurt or overly tired.

When all the calves were worked and branded, Stanley and Pat rode through the herd and found a couple of cows that had horns growing into their heads. This is a common problem in cows that have been dehorned. The horn sometimes comes back in a snaggled form and begins growing into the cow's head. If it isn't cut off, it can grow into the brain and kill the animal.

Stanley and Pat handled the cows with a roping technique I had never seen before, and which I thought was pretty slick. Stanley rode in and heeled the cow, catching her by both rear hocks. He turned his horse and started dragging her backward, and Pat rode in and heeled her front feet. They backed off, stretched her out on the ground, and held her by all four feet while several of us held her head and Kary Cox sawed off her horn.

I had been working on the river only a week, but already I had seen more good roping and good ropers than I had ever seen before.

It was just beginning to dawn on me what a useful piece of equipment the catch rope was, and that a cowboy who knew how to use it was far better and more useful in the pasture than one who didn't.

In skilled hands, the rope added a new dimension to cowboying. It gave a man options that he just didn't have without it.

Stanley Barby, getting ready to start heeling.

Chapter 5

Hobart and Carl

Through the rest of May and most of June, I rode on roundup crews. Every morning I would leave the house before daylight with a fresh horse in my trailer and drive anywhere from eight to thirty miles to join up with the crew. I spent a few days helping Stanley on the Bar B, but most of the time I was riding with the Open A crew.

The Open A was a big outfit and the operation was spread out over a wide area in Beaver and Harper Counties in the Oklahoma Panhandle. Five men worked full-time on the ranch, and they too were scattered. Darrell Cox, the foreman, lived outside of Rosston, at the east end of the ranch. Kary Cox, his son, who must have been about 21 then, lived nearby. Aaron Miller lived on the west edge of Knowles where the ranch had a set of shipping pens.

Hobart Hall lived about seven miles south of Knowles, and Carl Githens was located south of the river, five or six miles beyond Hobart's place, in what was called the Clear Lake Community.

Every morning, the Open A boys and I would meet at the assigned spot. One day we might gather at Mexico Creek on the south side of the river. The next day might find us at Knowles, and the next at Rosston.

The Open A was a classic study in the mobility of a modern cowboy crew. No matter where we met, someone had to drive for half an hour to get there. We put a lot of miles on our pickups that spring, and once we got there, we put a lot of miles on our horses.

It often happened that when we reached the meeting place at seven o'clock, we still had to haul the horses and crew several miles to the pasture. We would leave five or six pickup-trailer rigs sitting beside the highway and load all our horses into Darrell's big goose-neck trailer, which would hold nine horses. With the horses in the trailer, three cowboys in the cab of the pickup, and the rest of us in the back end, off we would go to begin the day's roundup work.

Working with the Open A cowboys day after day, I got to know them pretty well. I liked them all and enjoyed working with them, but I suppose if I had to choose one as my favorite, it would have to be old Hobart Hall.

Hobart didn't say a word to me the first week I was on the crew, and I decided that he was a grouchy old man. He certainly looked the part. He had short gray hair, cut in a flat-top style which gave him the bristled look of a porcupine. He wore a greasy felt hat, walked with a limp, rarely smiled, spoke in a gruff voice that sounded like a growl, and had a pair of narrow blue-gray eyes that reminded me of a snake or a lizard.

One morning we were working one of the pastures at Rosston. A grown bull cut back on us as we were driving the herd into the corral, and everyone but me and Hobart rode off into the hills to rope the bull and load him into a trailer.

We were alone, and there was an awkward silence between us. Then he darted his eyes toward me. "I hear you've got a book out."

"Yep." *Through Time And The Valley*, my first book, had just come out.

"Is it worth buying?"

"Nope."

"Good. I won't waste my money."

That broke the ice. From then on, Hobart and I were friends.

Hobart had been cowboying on the river for thirty years or more. He had started out working for the Old Gentleman, Otto Barby, on the original Barby Ranch, and when it had been split up, he had gone with Ralph Barby on the Open A.

He knew that whole country between Kiowa Creek and the Cimarron River. He knew every pasture by name and could tell you where the water and gates were located in every one of them. When we drove cattle across country, the boss would tell Hobart where he wanted us to leave the cattle, and Hobie acted as our guide and scout. He would point out the best and shortest route, and tell us where we would find the gates.

During the spring roundup of 1977, a big calf ran into a cutting gate that Hobie was operating. The gate hit him in the leg and shattered it badly. A year later, when I first met him, the leg was still giving him trouble. He walked with a limp and had a hard time getting on and off his horse—which, I think, explained why he always rode small horses.

On a chilly morning, when he crawled off his horse, he would stand on the ground for a minute or two, holding onto the saddle-horn while he tested the leg. He never complained about it, but I think it gave him a lot of pain. I tried to help him out when I could.

Open A cowboy Hobart Hall.

When I was riding with him and we came to a gate, I would always ride forward and open it. When we were driving stock together, I took the forward position and let him fall back on the drag, so that he wouldn't have to ride too hard.

Behind his gruff facade, Hobart had a good heart and a quick mind. He was the kind of man who could have done well in another line of work, but he had chosen the cowboy's life, I guess because he just liked it.

He was also the kind of man who drew pranks and teasing like a lightning rod, and there were several of us on the crew who spent most of our idle moments thinking of pranks to pull on him.

In May, the roundup crew spent a day working on the north end of the Bar B Ranch, sorting cattle in the Fry and Anderson pastures. We finished in the middle of the afternoon, and after we had put up our horses in our trailers, we sat around talking for a while. While Hobart was preoccupied, I slipped around and wired a tin can to the bumper of his pickup, so that it would drag the ground.

After a while, he and Carl Githens headed for home. They pulled onto the highway and were gabbing about something when Carl cocked his head and said, "Say, boy, I think you have a wheel bearing going out."

Hobart grumbled and pulled the rig off the road. He got out and went around checking all the wheels on the pickup and trailer, looking for a hot bearing. He didn't find one, so he started out again, creeping down the highway and listening.

He heard the sound and pulled off the road. This time he found the tin can. When he got back in, he said to Carl, "Wasn't a wheel bearing, just that damned John."

During the fall roundup season of 1978, I tormented Hobart on a regular basis. We started the fall work around the first of October and worked together as a crew until the middle of November. The weather was crisp and we were all full of hell and vinegar. I made it a standard practice to ride up behind Hobart while he was talking to someone, grab his horse's tail, dally it around my saddlehorn, and ride away, pulling his horse sideways.

I must have done this two dozen times before he decided to strike back. One morning, when he'd had enough of me, he rode up while I was talking to another man. He unsnapped the throat latch on my bridle and slipped the bridle off my horse's head, leaving me with no steering or whoa on a green-broke three-year-old mare.

That same mare—Calipso was her name—had a bad habit: any

time she got close to someone, she would start rubbing him with her nose. I decided to make the most of this. I would slip up behind Hobart when he was riding along and talking, and put my mare in position where she could rub on his leg.

He ignored this at first, but the mare kept at it and rubbed him so hard that she practically lifted him out of the saddle. Then he whirled around and roared at her. That fall, he came to hate that little mare, and any time he saw us coming toward him, he would pull down his rope and growl a warning.

One frosty morning, old Hobie had tanked up on coffee, and as we were riding to the back side of the pasture, he had to get down and relieve himself. He rode off to the side and turned his back on the crew while he took care of his business.

When I saw him out there, all spraddled out and helpless, I just couldn't resist the voice of Satan. I steered my mare toward him and stopped her just inches from his back. She went to rubbing on him, and every time she rubbed, she threw him forward several steps. He bellowed and squalled and threatened, while the rest of us almost fell out of our saddles laughing.

About fifteen minutes later, I was riding along and minding my own business. I heard horses coming up behind me and looked back over my shoulder. Hobart was riding toward me in a lope. Beside him and about twenty feet away was Kary Cox. They had Hobart's rope stretched between them, and their objective was to fit that rope under my mare's tail and get me bucked off.

I spurred Calipso and escaped, but for the rest of the day I didn't let Hobart out of my sight.

Hobart was the oldest member of the Open A crew—in his early sixties, I would guess. The next-oldest was Carl Githens. I never knew his age, but he was a grandfather and I would imagine that he was between fifty and fifty-five.

Hobart and Carl usually worked together and rode together. There were several similarities between them: both were older men, both were short, and both rode small paint horses. They belonged to the same generation and probably spent a lot of their time talking about the decline in the quality of cowboys, using me and the other younger guys as proof.

But in other respects, they were quite different. While Hobart tended to be brusk, taciturn, and satirical, there was nothing subtle or secretive about Carl. Whatever came to his mind, he said. In this respect they were an unlikely pair.

I still have a vivid memory of the two of them in Hobart's old

Open A cowboy Kary Cox.

red pickup. Hobart is slouched at the wheel, glaring at the road ahead, while Carl is puffing on the stump of a King Edward cigar and expounding on whatever subject is crossing his mind. As likely as not, Hobart is talking about one thing, Carl is talking about another, and neither is paying the slightest attention to what the other is saying.

Hobart once said, "You know the difference between Carl and a noisy radio? You can turn a radio off."

I got acquainted with Carl toward the end of the spring roundup season in 1978. Our crew had moved over to the Open A's country north of Knowles, a big stretch that ran all the way from Knowles to the Cimarron River. We were gathering cattle out of a big pasture that lay between the Cimarron and Tainter Creek, so named because it had once been the headquarters of the old Fred Tainter Ranch, one of the first of the big ranches in No Man's Land.

Carl and I were sent to the east side of the pasture. This country was rough and rocky, and since I didn't know the pasture or the roundup strategy, I stayed close to Carl so that I wouldn't get lost.

We rode for two hours and didn't see another soul. I don't think we were lost, because Carl knew those pastures very well, but he got to talking and one thing led to another, and I suppose he just lost track of the time and where we were.

In those two hours, we saw the back side of Beaver County, and I learned a lot about Carl's new dentures.

We were riding through a deep canyon, just west of Knowles Lake, when he pulled up his horse and stopped. He removed his upper plate, pulled a little can of denture adhesive out of the pocket of his leather jacket, and went to powdering his false teeth.

He told me that the teeth didn't fit right and that he had trouble talking. (This seemed an exaggeration.) He said that he had tried all kinds of adhesives, and that he carried paste in one pocket and powder in the other. Neither one of them seemed to work very well, and at the moment he was using powder on the top and paste on the bottom.

The day before, he went on, he had eaten a ham and cheese sandwich. The cheese had gotten balled up under the top plate and he had been forced to take it out and re-glue it.

The minutes stretched into hours. We rode up one canyon and down into another, and Carl talked on and on. Occasionally I would interject an "uh huh" or an "I'll be derned," while looking around and wondering what had become of the rest of the crew.

Finally we got out of the canyons and split up. Carl rode north

Open A Ranch foreman Darrell Cox, right, talks things over with
Hobart, left, and David Dunn.

and I rode south. By this time I had begun to wonder what kind of screwball roundup strategy we were following, and I started looking for cowboys, not cows.

I rode another half hour and found Pat Mason over on the west side. He asked where I had been and I said I wasn't sure. He told me the rest of the crew had moved on to another pasture and were heading toward the Cimarron.

Holding herd with Carl was always good for a laugh. It was a bit like sitting in the broadcast booth at a sporting event. Carl kept up a running commentary on the action and gave a play-by-play account of everything that was going on, something like this:

"There's a dry cow, that lineback with the snub horn. Get her, Stanley, I think she's dry. No, she may have a calf on her. She's got a pretty full bag and, let's see, turn around cow, yup, she's been sucked this morning, but where's her calf? She's wet but she hasn't found her calf, I guess. Better leave her.

"Well, there's one over here, this big yellow cow. Hey, here's a dry over here! Well, he's already got one, okay, bring her on. Watch her, boys, here she comes. Turn her, boys, bring her on, that's good. Get out of the herd, you old rip, it's getting hot out here."

As we used to say, Carl was quite a Carl and Hobart was quite a Hobart. Without those two on the roundup crew, life in cowboy country wouldn't have been nearly as much fun.

Erickson's work string on the John Little Ranch. From left: Star,
Honey, Ginger, Calipso, and Little John.

Chapter 6

The Horses

When I went to work on the LD Bar, I inherited a good string of horses that had been well trained by cowboys who had worked on the ranch before I got there. No matter which horse I chose for the day, I was well mounted. This made my work easier and more pleasant, and I owed my predecessors on the ranch a debt of thanks.

Cowboys come and go and move around from place to place. Over the years their names fade from memory. But they leave their mark on the horse herd. If they're good cowboys, they will leave the horses better than they found them. If they're not, they will leave behind horses that are soured and spoiled.

Nobody had to tell me that Pat Mason, Billy Joe Hansen, Jerry Coleman, and Ron Sallaska, cowboys who had worked on the ranch before I got there, were good hands, because they had left their signatures on the work string.

I had two ways of using my horses. The first was the rotation method. During the spring and fall roundup seasons, I rode every day for a month and a half or two months. These were long, hard days and I needed a fresh horse every morning. Under the rotation system, every horse would get several days of rest after each day of work. As a result, I never had trouble with horses going lame, losing flesh, or galling up.

During the roundup seasons, I kept the horses in a grass trap behind the corrals. Every morning around 5 o'clock, I whistled at them and they came into the barn, which had a stall for each horse. I fed each one a coffee can of rolled oats, with double rations for the horse I had worked the day before and double rations for the one I intended to ride that day.

While they ate, I went back to the house for breakfast, and when I returned to the barn, I kept up my mount for the day and turned the others out.

In the evening when I came home from work, I whistled them up again and gave them another feeding. Graining them twice a day kept them in top working condition, and it also provided me with a

Feed time.

painless way of catching a horse when I needed one.

The second method I used was more selective. When I had a specific job to do in the pasture, I tried to select the horse that I thought was best suited to it.

No two horses are exactly alike. Some are fast, some are slow. Some have good endurance and some don't. Some are stout and can pull a heavy load, and some aren't and can't. Some will buck on a frosty winter morning and some won't.

After you've ridden a horse a few times, you learn his strong points and his weaknesses, and since there is no one horse on earth that has all the qualities you want, you try to use each horse in the kind of work he does best.

For example, in the summer of 1978 I was out prowling in the bridge pasture, riding the young mare called Ginger. Near the windmill on the south end, I noticed a cow with a full bag. I rode around her and studied the signs and concluded that she had delivered a calf within the last 36 hours, but that the calf hadn't nursed.

Something was wrong and I needed to find out what it was.

When I made the sound of a bawling calf, she perked up her ears and looked off to the north. That told me where the calf was, so I got behind the cow and drove her in that direction. The farther we went, the faster she ran. Then she stopped in some tall grass and dropped her head. I rode to the spot and found the calf.

It was dead, and it appeared to me that it had been born prematurely, probably because the cow was old and in poor condition. We needed to get her out of the herd and sell her, and the best time to pick her out was right now, while there was no question about her identity.

I had known some cowboys and ranchers who probably could have memorized the cow and picked her out three months later, but I didn't trust my memory that far.

There were no pens or loading facilities in this pasture, and it was a long way back to the headquarters corrals. If I wanted the cow today, I would have to rope her and drag her into the stock trailer.

Since I was working alone, loading a grown cow in the pasture wouldn't be an easy job, and I sure wanted to have my best pulling horse to help. Ginger was a good little mare, but she didn't weigh much more than the cow and wasn't particularly good at pulling a load. So I went back to the house and saddled up old Star.

Star's main asset was his size, and his main liability was just the flip side: he had the size and strength but he was pretty slow. Adding it all up, I figured he had enough speed to give me a shot at the cow, and then enough stouts to drag her into the trailer.

I loaded him in the trailer and drove back to the bridge pasture. I tightened all my cinches and set the gates on the trailer so they would stand open. Then I rode toward the cow, who was grazing near the dead calf. I built a loop, put the spurs to Star, and the chase was on.

The cow outran Star at first, but I ran her in a big circle around the trailer until she wore down, then I roped her and brought her to a stop. I gave her a few minutes to fight the rope and to learn that she couldn't get away.

Star braced himself and stood his ground while she struggled. When the cow quit fighting, I slacked the rope, fell in behind her, and drove her toward the trailer. When she reached a point directly behind the open trailer gate, I eased her to a stop, flipped my rope over the racks, turned Star away from her, and told him to pull.

He put his 1300 pounds into the task and pulled her into the trailer, all but her hind legs. While she was catching her breath, I stepped down, ran around to the back of the trailer, and pushed her on in with the gate.

It didn't take me and Star long to do this job, but only because Star was stout enough to manhandle a grown cow. If I had tried to do it with a smaller horse, we might have gotten ourselves into a pulling match that we couldn't have won, and the job might have taken an hour or more.

Old Star wasn't a sprinter or a ballet dancer, but his ability to pull a load earned him a place in the work string. A man doesn't need or want five big plowhorses in his string, but he does need one that he can call on for heavy work.

The next horse in my string was Little John, the bay gelding who weighed somewhere between 1,000 and 1,100 pounds. Where Star was calm, slow, and a little lazy, Little John had great speed and a nervous disposition.

He was the hot rod of the work string. He excelled at calf roping in the pasture, and for that reason I often used him when I knew that I would have to doctor pinkeye. Jerry Coleman, who had worked on the LD Bar several years before I got there, had used Little John in the arena as a heading horse and had won some money on him, and he was well trained as a rope horse.

When you took down your rope and pointed him at a calf, he knew what was coming. He would start prancing, and when you

Scot talks things over with old Star.

turned him loose, he would take the bit in his teeth and go on the attack.

There wasn't an animal on the ranch that could out-run him, and he could catch up with a calf so quickly and put you up so close that it was a bit unsettling. It was nice to be riding a horse that gave you a good shot every time, but Little John went after cattle with reckless abandon, almost as though he wanted to eat them.

In the arena, that would have been just fine, because in the arena the stock has two good eyes and tends to run in a straight line toward the catch pen. And the ground is level and smooth. But out in the pasture, the conditions are quite different. The ground is *never* smooth and level, and most of the time I was going after calves that were blind or partially blind with pinkeye. You never knew which way they might turn, and they were as likely to run under the horse's feet as to cut in the other direction.

Little John didn't care. He loved the chase and didn't worry about doing cartwheels. But I did. I always figured that the best part of ranch roping was going home at night without any broken bones.

As a rope horse, Little John was just the opposite of Star. Star had trouble catching, but he could pull a house down once you had something on the string. Little John gave you the easy shots, but once you had caught, he lost all interest. Even though he had good size, he couldn't pull the bottom out of a wet paper sack. Maybe he hadn't been trained to pull or maybe he just had no taste for it, and if you spurred him to make him pull, he would either sull or start bucking.

For that reason, I used him strictly for calf roping and went out of my way to avoid roping grown stuff on him.

The next horse in the string was Ginger, a sorrel mare that was six or seven years old. I have spoken of both Ginger and Star as "sorrel" horses, which was the accepted description of their color in the Beaver River country. If we wanted to get technical about horse coloration and if we consulted that cantankerous expert on the subject, Ben K. Green, we would have to say that both horses were either "standard chestnut" or "bright chestnut."

"Sorrel," Green points out in his book, *The Color of Horses* (Northland Press, 1974), "is usually considered to belong to the draft horse breeds," and in the paintings that illustrate his text, he shows five Belgian horses as examples of the five shades of sorrel — no Quarter Horses at all.

So, to placate the ghost of old Doc Green, let us state for the record that Star and Ginger were chestnuts — and then go right on describing them as sorrels, because right or wrong, I never heard anyone on the river speak of a "chestnut" horse.

Ginger didn't have great size or speed or endurance, but neither did she have any glaring flaws. She made a good all-around ranch horse that could do a respectable job in all departments. She was pretty good at cutting, pretty good at roping, pretty good at pulling, and had better than average endurance.

The fact that she had no major flaws became her strongest point. When I wasn't sure what kind of work I might be doing, I could take Ginger and feel confident that we could get the job done. It might not be fancy, but we could do it well enough so that we wouldn't be ashamed of ourselves. And that earned her place in the string.

Then there was Honey, Ginger's mother. I never did like the looks of this dun mare. She was short-coupled and pot-bellied, and I just never did like a horse that was put together that way. Also, she had poor endurance and couldn't stand up to a hard day's work.

I never used her much in roundup season, when I might be in the saddle for 10 or 12 hours straight. But for short days and specific jobs, she could make a hand. She had good roping sense, didn't mind pulling a load, and she was the best cutting horse on the ranch.

If you didn't expect too much out of her, if you didn't push her beyond her physical limitations, she was willing and capable. But beyond a certain point, she ran out of gas and that was the end of it. You might as well have your saddle cinched up on a log.

The last horse in my string was the Calipso mare, an Anglo-Arabian that belonged to me. She was out of Mark Mayo's Egyptian stallion, Saturf, and a Thoroughbred mare that had done some running on the track. I had raised Calipso from a foal, broke and trained her myself, and no one else had ever ridden her.

She was a coming three-year-old in 1978 when I went to work on the Beaver River, and though she had been black at birth, she was beginning to show some grey in her coat. Among the cowboys, she was often referred to as "the little blue mare." By the time she reached the age of eight, she had become a dappled grey, much like her pappy, old Saturf.

During my first six months on the ranch, I used her only on a limited basis. I didn't want to push her too hard too fast. She still had a little bronc in her and wasn't yet mature physically.

I rode her several times during the 1978 spring roundup season, and that summer I began roping off her in the pasture. When the fall work started in October, I used her on several long, hard days and began easing her into the work string. In the spring of 1979, I worked her into the regular rotation and she earned her keep just the same as the other horses.

When I first started showing up on roundup mornings with the little blue mare, the other cowboys were amused. Anyone could see that Calipso would never make a cowhorse. She was too small and light-boned, which has always been regarded as the major deficiency of the Arabian horse, and one reason the Arabians have never won much respect among working cowboys.

I still remember Glenn Green's first comment about my little mare. We had finished a long day on the Open A's Cimarron country, and I was loading Calipso in the trailer. Glenn looked her over and said, "The little mare has guts, don't she."

I thought she did and I was pleased that Glenn recognized it.

"Yeah," he said, "takes guts to walk on them skinny laigs, let alone run."

That got a big laugh from the cowboys, who considered any horse under 1,000 pounds too small for cow work. Calipso weighed about 800 at that time.

I never claimed that she *looked* like a cowhorse, and Glenn was right about her skinny legs. She had the long legs of a running Thoroughbred, attached to a small Arabian body, with cat hams and a narrow chest. Standing beside the big Quarter Horses, she looked like a toy, entirely too frail and delicate for the hard life on a ranch.

The worth of any ranch horse lies in what he can do. Pedigree and appearance are important in the show ring but they don't mean much in the pasture. A horse that can perform and get the job done is a good horse—period. And little Calipso, skinny legs and all, could get the job done.

By the time she reached four years of age, she had become the best all-around ranch horse I had ever ridden. She had a soft mouth and a good handle. She was smooth and easy to ride in every gait. She had fairly good speed, she wouldn't cheat me in a roping situation, and she had the toughness and endurance that have always been the strong points of the Arabian breed.

She could lope mile after mile through sand and sagebrush and never hit bottom, and though I have heard that some lines of Quarter Horses are known for their endurance, I never worked around a Quarter Horse that could stay up with Calipso.

Modern cowboys who place so much emphasis on size and

Erickson and Calipso.

strength tend to forget that until the second or third decade of this century, virtually all ranch horses were small by today's standards. Most of them were probably near the size of Calipso—900 or 950 at maturity—and they did what had to be done. The West was won on small horses.

Which doesn't mean that small horses are better than big horses, or vice versa. That's an argument without end, and really, without much point. As a ranch cowboy who had many different kinds of work to do, I was glad to have both in my string.

Chapter 7

Prairie Fire

By the first of July, 1978, we had all the spring work finished. We had branded all the calves and moved the cows to summer pastures up and down the river, and I settled into a steady work routine on the LD Bar.

When I went to work on the ranch, John Little told me that he wanted his cattle ridden and checked twice a week, and so my summer routine was built around this. On Wednesdays and Saturdays I packed a lunch and a jug of water in the pickup, loaded my horse in the trailer, and headed north.

We had cattle located in four summer pastures that lay north of the river and were scattered over quite a large area. The bridge pasture was three miles east of headquarters. The Smith and Cosky pastures were up around Knowles, about ten miles from home. And the Charlie pasture was seventeen miles away.

When I prowled pastures I had several objectives in mind. I checked the water and salt, counted the cows, looked for strays and sick animals, and observed the general condition of the cattle and the grass.

I also went prepared to doctor for pinkeye. Doctoring pinkeye on a regular basis was something I had never done in my previous ranch jobs. (Some ranchers never doctor pinkeye, but let nature take its course. Their argument is that it takes too much time away from other jobs and it doesn't do much good anyway). On the Crown Ranch, I had doctored a few severe cases, but we hadn't had much of a problem with it while I was there. But 1978 must have been a bad year for pinkeye. We had a lot of it. Mr. Little wanted it treated and I fought it all summer.

Pinkeye is an inflamation of the eye which seems to affect Hereford, Hereford-cross, and white-face cattle more than other breeds, though the dark-eyed breeds are not immune to it. Some of the most severe cases of pinkeye I've ever seen were in black and black baldface steers.

The experts agree that pinkeye is caused by a virus, but what causes the virus to attack one animal and not another is subject to debate. Some think it is spread by flies. Others believe it's brought on by the glare of the sun, or weed pollen, or dust, or a combination of these.

It is most common in calves, though adult animals can get it too. A calf with a mild case of pinkeye will squint his eye and show a watery discharge on his face. While the disorder may cause him some discomfort, it doesn't impede his growth or affect his health.

But a bad case of pinkeye, especially when it settles in both eyes, can become a serious health problem. The eye can become so inflamed and ulcerated that the calf will go blind and the eyeball may burst, causing partial or complete blindness.

A blind calf may stop eating and drinking and lose his mother, and you're likely to find him off by himself, walking in circles. At best, he will become a thin, rough-haired runt that won't be fit to sell in the fall. At worst, he will die.

There were a number of medicines on the market that I had used to treat pinkeye: sprays, salves, powders, and even a solution that could be injected under the outer membrane of the eyeball. On the LD Bar, we used the old-time remedy: we threw a handful of stock salt into the inflamed eye. This method sounds harsh, but I don't know but what it worked as well as any of the drug store medicines.

When I rode pastures in the summer, I always carried a small bag of stock salt in my saddlebags.

But of course step one in this process was catching the calf, and that had to be done with the rope. That summer, I had to work hard at improving my roping skills, and I spent many hours in the evening and on Sunday afternoons practicing on the roping dummy in my front yard.

In the heat of the day, I could usually count on finding the cattle bunched up around a water hole or windmill. I would ride through the herd, trying not to disturb them and looking for pink-eye. When I spotted a bad-eyed calf, I would try for a quick easy shot in the herd.

Sometimes you can sneak up on the blind side of a calf and get the noose on him before he has a chance to run. That is by far the easiest way of doing it, and it saves all three parties (man, horse, and calf) a lot of sweat and effort.

But sometimes you miss that first throw, or sometimes the blind or half-blind calf is so wary that he won't let you get into throwing range, and then all you can do is ease him out of the herd

Erickson and friend Bill Ellzey spend a summer afternoon playing with their favorite toys, in the Ericksons' front yard at the Little Ranch.

Off to ride pastures in 100 degree heat.

and go after him. When the chase begins, you must rate the calf and wait for a shot, but you must also be aware of the terrain ahead, which might include brush, sandhills, ravines, holes, or trees.

Once you make the catch, you have to find the best way of putting the calf on the ground and getting him under control. Small calves are hard to catch but easy to handle. You throw a half-hitch over your dallies on the saddlehorn, run down the rope, and flank him down.

Bigger calves are easier to catch (they tend to run straighter and don't dodge as much, plus they're a bigger target to start with), but they're more difficult to put on the ground. If a calf is too big to flank down, then you either have to choke him down or trip him.

When you're roping pinkeyed cattle, you always have to remember that the beast you're chasing can't see very well, and sometimes he's stone blind. You don't always know where he's going. Since he can't see well, he reacts to sounds. If he hears a sound in front of him, which might come from other cattle or even from the echo of his own footsteps, he may cut away from the sound and run into the path of your horse.

When a horse gets a calf tangled up in his front legs, he's apt to fall, and his forward momentum can cause him to roll and do cartwheels, which is the kind of situation most cowboys try to avoid. You have to get close enough to the calf to give yourself a decent shot, yet hang back enough so that the little rascal won't trip up your horse.

The summer of 1978 turned out to be the hottest one on record. We went through a spell in July when the temperature stayed above a hundred degrees for two straight weeks. We'd had a good wet spring that had brought on the grass, but when the heat struck, everything shriveled up and turned brown in the pastures.

During that spell, it was nothing out of the ordinary for me to be out ahorseback in 105 to 108 degree heat. It was terrible! I would get so hot and dehydrated that every time I came to a windmill tank or pool of water, I would get down, soak my shirt, and put it on dripping wet. By the time I reached the next waterhole, it would be dry, and I would go through the process again.

It was during that spell that I learned to drink out of stock tanks. If the wind wasn't blowing, the windmills weren't bringing up fresh water, so I would part the moss on the surface of the tank and start drinking. I slurped it up through my teeth, to strain out all the bugs and vegetation. Well, one day in July I got back to the house about 7:00 in the evening—hot, dehydrated, blistered, burned, and worn to a nubbing. The temperature that afternoon had reached 106. I ate supper, took a cold bath, and was in bed asleep when the phone rang at 10:30.

It was Mrs. Little up at the big house. She said that she and Mr. Little had just driven in from Beaver and had discovered a prairie fire on the Three Cross Ranch, north of our place. Lightning had struck in pasture #3, about two and a half miles north of us, and the dry grass and sagebrush were on fire.

The wind had shifted to the north and it was burning our way.

Mr. Little was sounding the alarm on the two-way radio, and she was calling other ranches on the phone.

Mrs. Little was 75 years old, a very sweet and pretty little lady who had been raised on that ranch and was as tough as iron. I thought she had a cute way of telling me to get out of bed and go fight the fire. She said, "I just thought you might want to know about the fire."

As a matter of fact, I didn't want to know. I wanted to sleep. But I jumped into my clothes, told Kris that I didn't know when I would be back, and ran to the barn. I gathered up an arm-load of gunny sacks, threw two shovels into the back of the pickup, and went roaring up the hill.

I turned on the two-way radio, which was hooked up to four ranches along the river, and heard conversations between several mobile units and base stations, as cowboys and ranchers called in to check the location of the fire. Like me, they had left a nice comfortable bed to go fight the fire.

I didn't need anyone to tell me where the fire was, because as soon as I drove out of the trees in the hollow, I could see the glow reflected on the dark clouds overhead. The night was pitch black. There was no moon, no stars, no lights of any kind, just that undulating orange glow on the clouds.

About two miles north of headquarters, I topped a sandhill and saw the fire itself. Flames were leaping up from the dry sagebrush, and the farther I drove, the bigger it seemed to grow.

When I arrived on the scene, I didn't see any men or pickups. It appeared that there were only two living things out there in the night: me and the fire. I could hear the fire roaring and popping.

I didn't know what to do, so I stopped in the road and got out. I wasn't anxious to pick up a gunny sack and run out to fight the fire. Then I heard voices and saw a pickup out in the pasture. I threw my pickup into four-wheel drive and headed across the sandhills toward the other vehicle.

Stanley Barby and his son Rodney had beat me there, and so

had Leland Barby. As I drove closer, I could see them swinging gunny sacks. I jumped out, wet down two sacks, and joined them on the fire line.

Within minutes, other pickups arrived, and more men came with sacks. We yelled orders back and forth and never did know to whom we were speaking because we couldn't see faces in the dark.

The fire burned down a sandhill and we succeeded in putting out the flames when it reached a sandy draw that didn't have much vegetation on it. Unless the wind came up and spread the sparks to another location, we had it under control. Now all we had to do was go back through the burned area and make sure that all the glowing cow chips and sagebrush stumps were extinguished.

We put our sacks away and went to work with shovels, throwing sand on the embers.

Now that we were fighting sparks instead of flames, I had a chance to look around and see some of the men I had been working beside for the last hour: Stanley and Rodney Barby, Leland Barby, Read Barby, Lloyd Barby (if you ever want to meet some Barbys, just go to the Beaver River and yell *fire* real loud); Pat Mason, Billy Rose, and several other men I didn't know.

There must have been ten or twelve men fighting the fire. They had all reached the scene less than twenty minutes after the alarm had gone out, and they had all traveled over rough country roads to get there. It appeared to me that we had a pretty salty fire department on the river.

By 11:30 we had the fire whipped. We had been lucky. Had the wind come up suddenly or shifted directions, we might have lost it. If that had happened, we might have been out all night, and we might have been forced to sound a general alarm, calling in county fire trucks and heavy equipment. If the fire had burned south and gotten into the meadows and timber along the river, it would have been very bad.

We gathered around Stanley's pickup and passed around a jug of water. I had worked up a burning thirst and that water sure tasted good. We talked for a while and watched the clouds. The worst of the lightning had moved off to the southeast, and we waited to see if it would start any more range fires.

It didn't, and we said good night and went back to our home ranches.

I got home around midnight and, since I smelled and looked like burned garbage, I had to take another bath. When I finally crawled between the sheets, nobody had to rock me to sleep.

Jake and some of his admirers before the rodeo.

Chapter 8

Jake Parker

During the summer months, I spent most of my time working alone, riding fence, repairing windmills, and prowling pastures. This wasn't very exciting work, and I looked forward to the time when the days grew shorter, the nights turned crisp and chilly, and the trees began to turn along the river.

That would signal the approach of fall and the big fall roundup season, when all the cowboys on the river would reassemble and work together as a crew.

It was Jake Parker who got the fall roundup season kicked off, took me off the posthole digger and put me ahorseback where I belonged. One day in September, he drove over to the LD Bar and asked if I could help him for a few days.

Jake was the foreman of Leland Barby's Three Cross Ranch, and he headquartered on the river just a mile west of us. Since Jake and I were close neighbors and enjoyed working together, we had a regular swap-out arrangement, where I would help him with his jobs and he would help me with mine. The deal worked well for both sides, and I was always delighted to have a chance to work with him.

People who knew Jake often came up with the same description of him: he was a natural-born cowboy. If you took all the qualities that have made the American cowboy an enduring character in our folklore, threw them into a gunny sack, shook them up, and poured them out on the ground, you would have Jake Parker.

He was a skilled and patient horseman, a deadly roper, and a good judge of cattle. He loved his work, had a big heart, and didn't know how to tell a lie—well, a dishonest lie. He was a man of quiet courage, he was a great storyteller whose sense of humor was deeply rooted in the earth, and he had a pleasant, easy-going disposition.

I guess Jake was around 45 years old at this time, or maybe 50. He did the work of a young man and he had a young buck's enthusiasm for the cowboy life. The quality that showed his age the most was not his gray hair or wrinkles, but the manner in which he paced himself.

That's a quality a man acquires with age. A young man tends to squander his energy and to fly into every job like a buzz saw. Jake didn't operate that way. He had worked 12- and 14-hour days most of his life and he had learned to save something for the end of the day.

In the morning, his pace seemed slow, but by the end of the day he was still working when the young bucks were ready to head for the barn.

Also, he didn't take unnecessary chances. He had reached the age where he didn't heal up as fast as he once had, and he had figured out that the smart cowboy sees a wreck before it happens. When he had to tackle a risky job and take chances, he would do it because that was part of the job, but you always had the feeling that he had calculated the odds and knew what he was getting into.

Some older guys will push the high-risk jobs off on the younger men — roping a wild cow or being the first to cross the river where it may be hiding quicksand. Jake wasn't that kind. When a bunch of us younger guys were helping him on the Three Cross, he always dealt himself the hardest, dirtiest, most dangerous assignments.

He stood six feet tall and was of medium build, neither heavy nor thin. He always wore faded jeans, an old pair of boots that had been patched to fit his corns, and a long-sleeved western shirt. I can't remember ever seeing him out in the pasture with a cowboy hat. He preferred a cap to a hat — a Scotch cap with ear flaps in the winter, and a plain old give-away cap in the summer.

I don't know what he had against cowboy hats, whether they had gotten too expensive for him or if he had decided that a cap was a more practical kind of headgear in the windy Panhandle.

Jake was a man who had never gotten anything the easy way. Everything he owned he had worked for. And he worked very hard. He always had some little deal going on the side as a way of making extra money for his family, which included his wife Audrey and three daughters. While he was foreman of the Three Cross, he ran a few cattle of his own, broke and rode outside horses, day-worked for other people on Sundays and holidays, and during the summer months, he worked as a pickup man for the Barby Rodeo Company.

I had seen Jake at work in the rodeo arena several years before I ever met him. In 1975 I attended a rodeo in Beaver. Lloyd Barby was the stock contractor for the show, and Jake was one of the pickup men. I had never paid much attention to the pickup men at a rodeo, but at this performance I found myself watching them.

A young cowboy came out on a bareback bronc and rode him to the whistle. When he heard the whistle, he grabbed the rigging with both hands and hung on. The pickup men, Jake Parker and Read Barby, moved in from both sides and Jake got close enough so that the kid could bail off.

Up in the stands, I could hear Jake telling him to get off the bronc before he got thrown. But the kid was scared and wouldn't let go.

By this time the bronc had bucked across the arena and had come to the fence. There, he whirled to the left and started running down the fence as hard as he could go. If the kid came off now, he would get himself splattered all over the fence.

Read was on the right side and got squeezed out between the bronc and the fence. He dropped back, and that left Jake to work alone. He spurred his big sorrel horse into a gallop and started after the bronc.

When he pulled abreast of the bucking horse, he reached out, threw an arm around the boy's mid-section, and at 30 or 35 miles an hour, yanked him off the bronc and set him safely on the ground.

The crowd applauded the bronc rider, but my eyes followed Jake, who was now riding at top speed after the bronc and leaning out of the saddle to unhook the bucking cinch around its flanks. Later in the evening, when it was time for the bull riding, Jake and Read were in the arena again, this time to run the bulls into the catch pen and clear the arena after each ride. The first three or four bulls left without an argument, but the next one, a big black horned bull, decided he wasn't going to leave.

Jake and Read chased him around and gave him several chances to go to the catch pen. Instead, he turned, lowered his head, and made a pass at one of the horses. Jake already had his rope down. He swung the loop over his head, dropped it over the bull's neck, dallied up to the horn, and headed for the catch pen in a lope.

The bull braced all four feet against the rope, and Junior, Jake's favorite arena horse, sledded him all the way to the catch pen. Two minutes later, the show went on. Before the performance was over, Jake had one-looped three more bulls and hauled them out of the arena.

He made this look so easy that an inexperienced observer might have thought that anyone could rope and drag an 1800 pound fighting bull. I knew better. Any man who goes around roping rodeo bulls is either a little bit crazy or a heck of a cowboy.

When you stick a rope on a grown bull, you have to figure that there are five or six things that can happen, and only one of them is good. The rest of them can be mighty hard on clothes. But that didn't bother Jake. He roped bulls because that was part of his job, but I also think that he enjoyed it. I asked him about this one day and he admitted it.

"If you've got the horse for it, it can be fun," he said with typical modesty. Jake's idea of fun and mine were not the same. I admired his skill, but he didn't need to worry about me applying for his job.

One time I found a Hereford bull in the bridge pasture that had bad feet and needed to go to the sale barn. We didn't have any pens or loading facilities in that pasture, so the only way of putting wheels under him was to rope him and load him into the trailer. Since we had a bull-roping expert on the next ranch, I went over to the Three Cross and borrowed Jake and Buck, a big dun horse he had recently bought.

We rode out into the pasture and found the old bull on the south end. Jake drove him up to the trailer, tossed a loop around his horns, and had the old fellow loaded in a matter of minutes.

"Parker," I yelled at him, "you make that look a whole lot easier than it really is."

He laughed. "Well John, he's just some old cow's calf."

Well, that was typical Jake Parker. He was one of those guys from Cowboy Country who could teach a young feller something about the cowboy business. And when he came to the ranch that day in September and gave me a good excuse for putting away the posthole diggers, I was delighted.

The next morning, I saddled Calipso and trailered over to the Three Cross. Leland Barby, the owner, had built a fine set of pens about half a mile north of the river. They were made of welded pipe and landing mats, with corner posts cemented into the ground. These pens were substantial enough to hold any kind of animal. On the west side of the pens, he had five or six sheltered horse runs, with a feed room, a tack room, and a little office nearby.

His cattle-working facilities lay to the east of the horse runs: an alley, four sorting pens, and a loading chute made of concrete and steel. And then on the south side, he had a big arena where, in years past, he had held ropings and cutting contests.

As the rest of the crew pulled in, it occurred to me that, of the seven cowboys on the crew that day, I would be the only one who had never competed in rodeo. There was Del Roy Spurgeon, a tall

Read Barby and Jake carrying in the colors. Minutes later, they were
picking up bronc riders. They are wearing padded chaps to protect
their legs.

handsome young man with a bright red mustache and an easy smile, who grew up on the Cimarron River and came from a long line of rodeo people. He was a regular competitor in amateur rodeos and team ropings. He had brought a friend named Bill, who was also a roper.

The other four men—Jake, Read Barby, Guy Paine, and Tommy Cochran—had competed in amateur rodeo and were also part-time employees for the Barby Rodeo Company. Read rode bulls and bareback broncs and worked in the arena with Jake as a pickup man. Guy Paine was a bull rider and pickup man, and Tommy Cochran rode bareback broncs and helped care for Barby's bucking stock at the shows.

Back around the turn of the century, ranching and rodeo were virtually the same. A rodeo performer was a ranch hand who had better than average skills. That close relationship between pasture and arena is rare in the present day, but it was still alive on the Beaver River in 1978, where ranching and rodeo came together in the Barby Rodeo Company.

Chapter 9

The Barby
Rodeo Company

At least two places in Texas, Pecos and Canadian, make the claim that rodeo began in their towns in the late 1880s. The argument over where rodeo began probably won't be resolved any time soon, but there is no argument over how and why rodeo got started: a bunch of ranch cowboys got together one day and decided to find out who could rope and ride the best.

The first American rodeos weren't the spectator events they are today. They had crude facilities, no grand entry, and little or no prize money. Since it wasn't actually a sport in the beginning, there was no such thing as a professional rodeo performer. Those who competed were ranch hands, and the events tested skills that were used in pasture work every day.

Over the years, rodeo evolved into a sport and its connection to ranching became more remote. By the second or third decade of this century, the term "rodeo hand" had become something of a slur to ranch owners and managers, who didn't have any use for that breed of young men who practiced their roping and bronc riding on ranch stock.

Even at this early date, cattlemen perceived that the aims of ranching and rodeo were not the same, and perhaps not even compatible.

Today's professional rodeo continues to draw young people with ranch backgrounds, yet the competition has become so intense and specialized that it bears only a faint resemblance to what occurs in ranch work. The day has passed when a cowboy could walk off a ranch in Montana, enter the bronc riding in Cheyenne, and expect to finish in the money.

Today's rodeo champions are professional athletes, and those who win consistently have more than raw talent. The qualities that make them champions (self-discipline, physical conditioning, and constant practice) are developed in the arena, not in the pasture. Indeed, the modern professional rodeo performer may have more in common with professional soccer players than with ranch cowboys, even though rodeo performers continue to think of themselves and describe themselves as cowboys.

The division between ranching and rodeo is not quite as clear once you drop down into amateur rodeo circles, where a ranch cowboy can still compete in a week-end rodeo now and then without being humiliated by the competition. It's still rodeo, not ranch work, but at least he's competing against other part-timers who have jobs and families and can't spend eight hours a day honing their skills in the arena.

One of the things that interested me about the cowboys I met on the Beaver River was that virtually *all* of them had had amateur rodeo experience, and most of them were still entering rodeos when I met them in 1978. There was no strict division or hostility between ranch and arena. Cowboys who competed in the arena on Saturday were back in the pasture Monday morning, and so were their horses.

In other words, the same balance between work and fun which was present at the very first rodeos still existed on the Beaver River. I had been involved in ranch work long enough to know that this easy movement from pasture to arena didn't exist in many places. Most of the ranch owners I knew didn't approve of rodeo. Or to put it more accurately, they enjoyed watching rodeo as a sport but didn't want their own cowboys involved in it. In their minds, rodeo was something you did in town, not in the country.

So why were the Barby ranches different? It certainly didn't originate in the Old Gentleman, Otto Barby Sr. Of course I never knew the man, but I gathered from stories about him that he was a stern German who believed in work and more work. I would guess that at the time he was putting his ranch together, ranchers of his generation had gone sour on ropers and rodeo cowboys, probably because they had seen too many cattle killed and crippled, too many horses ruined by young men who had their minds on the arena.

It was Otto Sr.'s grandson, Lloyd Barby Jr., who brought rodeo to the Beaver River country. Lloyd and his wife Ruth lived at the west end of the Barby country, about five miles upriver from where we lived on the John Little ranch, and we passed near their house every time we drove into town.

Lloyd grew up on the old ranch, when times were hard and every major decision was made by the Old Gentleman. I once heard someone say that when Lloyd crawled out of his cradle, he crawled on a horse and went straight to the pasture. As a boy, he did a man's work.

Lloyd Barby, owner of the Barby Rodeo Company.

Guy Paine: bull rider, pickup man, and ranch cowboy.

They tell about the time Lloyd took a flatbed truck down into Texas to get a load of hay. When he reached the hay field, he had to do some work on the truck motor, and while he was working, one of his fingers got cut off in the fan belt. He wrapped the stump in a rag and finished loading the truck, drove back to the ranch and stacked the hay in a barn. Then he went to the house to take care of his finger.

In 1964 Lloyd built a small rodeo arena at his ranch north of the river. He brought in a few old range cows and sour horses, and every Friday night he held a "fun night" for his family and cowboys. Everyone had such a good time bucking out the ranch stock that he began bringing in a few outside bulls and horses with proven bucking ability.

To help pay the feed bills, he started putting on junior rodeos and furnishing the stock. One thing led to another, and by 1966 when he produced the Block and Bridle rodeo at Oklahoma State University, he was not only a cattle rancher but also a rodeo stock contractor.

By 1977 the Barby Rodeo Company had two semi-trucks hauling stock to five states and putting on sixty performances a year. The Barby string had grown to 45 bucking bulls, more than a hundred broncs, and 35 head of corriente steers for bulldogging and roping.

In amateur rodeo circles, the Barby name meant quality: good fresh bucking stock, pickup men who were knowledgeable and skilled, and people who were honest in their dealings with the cowboys and the local rodeo committees. It was a family business, involving Lloyd, his wife Ruth, daughter Jan and her husband Guy Paine, and son Read.

Read was around thirty, and he and his wife Jerry Lynn lived on the south side of the river, a couple of miles from Lloyd and Ruth's place. Read worked with the rodeo company in the summers, hauling stock in one of the semi-trucks and working in the arena as a pickup man.

Though he was involved in putting on the rodeos, he usually found time to compete in the bronc riding and bull riding. He got no special favors from the stock, just because he fed and cared for them. He won his share of prize money but also ate his share of dirt.

In the off-season, he worked with Lloyd on the ranch and at the Beaver Livestock Auction, shoed horses, plaited bull-riding ropes, ran a trapline, and taught a Sunday school class in Beaver.

In 1978 Read brought honor to our neighborhood when he was

Read Barby, ready to go to work on rodeo night.

named one of the three outstanding young men in Oklahoma. When asked how it felt to be living with a celebrity, his wife said, "Oh, it's wonderful, but he still leaves his dirty socks in the living room."

Very few people ever see a rodeo from the perspective of the stock contractor, and many people don't understand what he does. He signs a contract with the local rodeo committee and furnishes the bucking and roping stock, the pickup men, the pickup horses, and a basic crew of skilled hands who know how to put on a rodeo.

He may also hire the bullfighters, clowns, and novelty acts.

The stock contractor's primary objective is to put together a string of bulls and horses that will buck hard every time the chute gate is opened. Since rodeo riders are scored on the difficulty of the ride and can't place in the money unless the animal performs well, they want rank stock, and their opinion of the contractor will depend on the quality of his animals.

Rodeo is often viewed as a contest between man and beast, but it's also a contest between cowboys and the stock contractor. In many ways the contractor is like the conductor of an orchestra. He has spent years buying, culling, testing, and developing huge animals who have only one task to perform.

On rodeo night they are turned out into the arena for eight seconds, and during that short span of time they are expected to throw some young cowboy into the dirt. The contractor's reputation will stand or fall on how well they perform that task.

During a rodeo performance, Lloyd was at work behind the chutes. He was a study in concentration. He knew the habits and personalities of every bull and horse in his string. He knew which horses were flighty in the chute, which ones might sull at a premature spurring, and which ones should be turned out fast.

Standing above the chutes, he gave instructions to the gate man and the rider. During the bull riding, he told the clown which bulls would fight, which way they were likely to turn, and what the clown might do to improve the bull's performance. Sometimes, after the ride had begun, he shouted the animal's name over and over. He had learned that some bulls perform better at the sound of their names.

Handling bucking stock is both an art and a science, and it is also dangerous. "Every horse and bull has a personality," Lloyd once said. "We have to know which horses will kick and which bulls will fight. Putting on a rodeo is as dangerous as contesting in one.

The contractor is subjected to every animal, while the contestant is subjected only to one."

Lloyd knew what he was talking about. In one two-year span, he suffered two broken arms from fighting bulls, almost lost an ear to a flying chute gate, and was run over and knocked unconscious by a bucking horse.

Putting on rodeos was a rough way to make a living, but the Barbys seemed to enjoy it and thrive on it. Typical of the cowboy breed, Lloyd took his lumps with a sense of humor:

"The most dangerous part of this business," he once said, "is trying to get out of the rodeo grounds without running over a beer bottle."

Chapter 10

The Fall Work

During the month of September, I spent a lot of time ahorseback. I helped Jake and Leland on the Three Cross and they came over and helped me attend to a few chores.

We usually worked small crews of four to seven men. The big fall roundup season didn't start until the first of October, when the Open A and the Bar B got cranked up. Then we were going every day, rounding up, sorting, and shaping up the cattle for fall shipping.

Our average crew then was twelve cowboys, though sometimes we had more. Each day we worked a different pasture. We gathered the cattle, separated the dries from the wets, moved the dries to winter range, and moved the cows with calves into traps and small pastures near shipping pens, so that on shipping day we could gather them quickly, cut off the calves, push them across the scales, and load them into trucks.

I had been working on the river for five months by this time, yet I still had a hard time keeping all the pastures straight in my mind. We were working such a big stretch of country, and there were so many pastures involved, I often had to ask Hobart or one of the veteran cowboys how to get to the pasture we had been assigned to work.

My outfit, the LD Bar, was small and fairly simple. We had the horse pasture, the west meadow, middle meadow, east meadow, bridge pasture, Cosky, Smith, and Charlie pastures.

The Three Cross was more complicated. South of the river there were the black cow pasture, Duck Pond Creek, and several small pastures and wheat fields. North of the river, the Three Cross had a big chunk of country: pastures 2, 3, 4, 5, 5½, and 6, the horse pasture, the home meadow, west meadow, and the heifer pasture.

The Bar B joined the Three Cross on the west, and it had another list of pastures: the river pasture, the Huff place, Healy timber, bull pasture, buffalo pasture, prairie dog town, the Anderson place, and the Fry place. Ten miles downriver, Stanley had another ranch called the Allen place. It was divided into four pastures and three fields, and I never did learn the names of those pastures.

Then, of course, there was the Open A which had pastures all over the country. The ones I remember are pastures 1 and 7, Mexico Creek, Chambers Lake, Rutherford, Rosston west, Rosston east, Rosston middle, Rosston bull, Rosston river, Knowles, Cimarron River, and Tainter Creek.

Even though this list is incomplete, you can see the problem. I knew the name and location of about forty pastures, and there must have been another twenty that I couldn't name.

In the fall, the morning air was crisp and fresh. We hit the saddles right after sunup and had to carry enough clothes to keep ourselves warm in the event that a norther came whistling down while we were out. Once we left the pickups and trailers at sunup, there was no going back. What we wore in the morning was what we had for the rest of the day.

We never knew what to expect from the weather at that time of year. The afternoon temperature might climb into the eighties or it might be down around the freezing mark. I always carried plenty of clothes, and usually I would start peeling them off around ten o'clock. I would finish the day with a slicker, jacket, leather vest, and maybe even a flannel shirt tied to the saddle strings.

Most of the cowboys on our crew wore leather leggings in the fall and didn't take them off unless we had to get down and do some work afoot. When the temperature climbed into the eighties, we boiled in our leggings. They were too hot to wear, but a guy didn't dare go out without them.

We all paid close attention to the weather forecast in the fall. The weatherman wasn't always right, but he usually gave us advance warning when a major change was on the way.

One morning toward the end of October, we were supposed to meet at the Open A's pasture #1, southwest of Knowles. Jake Parker picked me up around eight. The day was sunny and warm, and I went dressed for moderate weather.

I loaded my horse in the trailer and we started north. When we had gone a mile or so, Jake looked me over and said, "Are you sure you've got enough clothes? They said on the radio that we're supposed to get a cold norther before noon."

I had missed that. We turned around and went back to my place. I put on a pair of one-piece long johns, traded my felt hat for a wool cap, and pulled on a pair of lined gloves.

Half an hour after we had hit the saddles, I started pulling off clothes and tying them to the saddle strings. I was about to roast. While we held herd, I yelled at Parker and told him his weatherman didn't know what he was talking about.

The words were hardly out of my mouth when I glanced off to the north and saw a dark line of dust and clouds creeping up the horizon. Before long, we were hit by a blast of cold air. My mare started bucking and I started putting my clothes back on.

An hour after the norther hit, we twelve cowboys were humped up in a wind-driven snow.

Over the howl of the wind, I yelled to Jake, "Say, you sure have a smart weatherman!"

Several days later, we moved over to Rosston and worked the big 6,000 acre river pasture. While we were holding herd, I noticed that the man to my right was new. I had never seen him before. He didn't look comfortable on his horse, and he wasn't watching the cattle. I guessed that he was somebody's friend, maybe a man from town who had come out to ride with us.

There was a big red heifer on the edge of the herd, one of those wild brushy critters that had escaped us in the spring. She weighed around 600 pounds, yet she had never been branded or dehorned.

We had flushed her out of the tamaracks and now she had seen enough of the daylight and was ready to go back to the river.

The man to my right wasn't watching her, but she was watching *him*. And pretty soon she had him figured out. All at once she threw up her tail and bolted the herd. The man never saw her coming, and by the time he had plow-reined his horse, she was gone.

I waited to see what he would do about it. Under the unwritten cowboy code, he who maketh a mistake payeth the consequences. He'd let her go, and bringing her back should have been his problem.

But if he was someone's guest, the rules didn't apply. I located Stanley Barby, who was cutting in the herd, and caught his eye. He nodded. I turned Star, left the herd, and went after the heifer.

I caught up with her and turned her north, away from the brush. I tried to point her back to the herd but she wouldn't go. When she cut back on me the third time, I built a loop, fell in behind her, and caught her around the horns on the first shot.

When I got her stopped, I noticed that I was only about fifty yards from the herd. If I had missed the shot or made a sloppy job of it, every man on the crew would have seen it, which would have been rather humiliating. I mean, a guy doesn't mind throwing loops into the dirt when he's off by himself, but in front of his peers . . . no.

Jake Parker and Buck put the string on a cow. As usual, Parker needed only one loop.

If I had thought of that during the run, I probably would have choked up, but I hadn't. I'd made a perfect run in front of a crowd, and that didn't hurt my reputation.

This old heifer was in a hostile mood and fought against the rope. She didn't give me an inch of slack, and it suddenly occurred to me that my saddle was moving.

I hadn't remembered to take up my latigo.

With a loose cinch, I couldn't risk dragging the heifer back to the herd, since in the process I might have ended up with my saddle around Star's buttocks, which ain't the ideal place.

Stanley saw my problem and loped out on his big black horse. He pitched his rope on top of mine, and while he held the heifer, I got down and tightened up my cinches.

Stanley decided we'd better stick the old sister in a trailer, or else she'd be giving us trouble all day. He pulled her from the left side and I pulled her from the right, and we spurred our horses and headed for the nearest trailer.

The heifer set all four feet against the rope and didn't walk a step, and we gave her a ride she didn't forget. Her feet hit the ground about once every ten feet, and she didn't get any more chances to play outlaw.

After lunch, we split the crew. One bunch drove cows with steer calves up north to the middle pasture, while the other took cows with heifer calves up to the bull pasture. I went with Stanley's crew.

Half an hour after we left the roundup ground, we were pushing our herd through some high sandhills. I was up near the front of the herd, backing up Glenn Green who was riding the point.

These old river cows had some run in them and Glenn was having to pinch them pretty tight on the point to hold them back. I watched every move he made and was there to back him up.

At last we got the run out of them and had them strung out in a long line. Glenn stopped old Moose on top of a sandhill and I rode up beside him. He was looking off to the south toward a cloud of dust.

I looked closer to see what had caused the dust and saw cattle and cowboys flying over the hills. The other crew had run into some trouble and were in the middle of a stampede.

Glenn said, "Looks like they're exercising the cattle." And then he turned Moose and rode on.

Scot Erickson, age four, and Hopi.

Chapter 11

Shipping Time

My boss, John Little, decided that he wanted to ship the LD Bar calves to the Beaver Livestock Auction on Wednesday, October 11. Several days before the appointed day, I began making preparations. I called all the cowboys from Rosston to Barby Bridge and lined up a crew of eleven men.

All of our shipping calves were located in one pasture, which we called the bridge pasture because a pipeline bridge crossed the river down on the south end. We didn't have a set of shipping pens in the bridge pasture, so on Monday I cornered Jake Parker and Guy Paine and we spent an afternoon setting up a portable corral with a loading chute. We built it near an oil field road so that Lloyd Barby's trucks could come and go without getting stuck in the sand.

Tuesday evening, everything was set, but just to be certain, I drove over to the pasture and walked around the pens, making sure there weren't any weak spots and that all the gates were set.

On shipping day, you have a lot of things on your mind and decisions that have to be made quickly, and it's easy to make little mistakes that can be embarrassing. This was my first shipping roundup on the Little ranch, and I didn't want to make any slip-ups.

That night, I set my alarm for five o'clock and went to bed early so that I would get a good night's sleep. I got a good night's sleep all right. My alarm didn't go off and I woke up at seven o'clock.

I had ordered trucks for 9:00 and had told the crew to be at the pens at 7:30 sharp. I had exactly 30 minutes to catch, feed, saddle, and load my horse, and drive three miles to the pens — and, if I could work it in, put on some clothes before I got there.

I flew out of bed like a scalded cat, grabbed a banana for breakfast, and ran to the barn. I scared old Star so badly that it took me five minutes to get a bridle on him. I finally got him cornered, stuffed the bit into his mouth, threw a saddle on him, jerked the cinches down so hard he grunted, led him to the trailer, slapped him on the butt, slammed the gate, jumped into the pickup, and gave that poor horse one of the wildest rides through the hills that he ever got.

And then I ate my banana.

I drove up to the pens in the bridge pasture at exactly 7:32. I was late to my own roundup! Ten cowboys stood around smirking. I knew what was coming.

Hobart was grinning like an alligator. "Where you been, Jawn? I got up at five o'clock so's I wouldn't be late to your roundup." And so on and so forth. Hobart squeezed it for all it was worth, and there was nothing I could say.

Several days later, we moved over on the Bar B and started gathering Stanley's cattle and shipping the calves. That fall, Stanley had an old man working for him named Slim. I guess he had a last name but I never heard it. He was probably somewhere between 65 and 70, and most of the time he stayed around headquarters and took care of the horses and the chores.

Because of Slim's age, Stanley didn't work him very hard or use him much in pasture work, but that fall he needed an extra rider so he put Slim ahorseback.

He was a funny-looking old bird on a horse. He had a big belly and pipe-cleaner legs, and he always wore bib overalls and a cap. He sat straight up in the saddle and rode like a sack of potatoes. He rarely got his horse out of a walk, and when he did, he bounced up and down and flopped his elbows. He rode with his head down and didn't pay much attention to what was going on around him.

Old Slim wasn't much of a cowboy, didn't pretend to be, and probably wished he was back at the house doing the chores.

He was a snuff-dipper—a *real* snuff-dipper. Instead of using Skoal or Copenhagen, as many of the cowboys did (which, strictly speaking, isn't actually snuff), Slim used the old-fashioned brown powder that was nothing but straight tobacco—no syrup, no sweeteners, no mint or wintergreen.

And when he loaded up with Levi Garrett, you wanted to keep your eye on him and pay attention to which way the wind was blowing, because, as Glenn Green warned, "Slim can drown a goose."

This became a matter of genuine concern when the crew traveled to and from the house at dinnertime. We all went to the house in one pickup. Slim and Hobart were the senior members of the crew, so they got to ride in the cab, while the rest of us piled in the back end.

Slim always sat by the window, and every time he turned his face to spit, someone sounded the alarm and we started ducking.

I remember one hot afternoon when we had been out in Stanley's dogtown pasture and came into the pens. We were all hot and dry, and we headed straight to the big water can that Stanley carried in the back of his pickup.

Slim and I arrived there about the same time, and since he was the older man, I showed my respect by handing him the drinking cup. This cup was a Stanley Barby invention: a rusted bean can with a baling wire handle.

Slim filled the cup and drank, then he sighed and grinned and handed it to me. "Sure is good," he said.

I took the cup and drank, and tried to forget the brown ring of snuff juice under Slim's lower lip.

By the middle of November, my outfit still had about 70 head of cows up north on summer pasture, and since it was getting late in the season, we decided to move them down to winter pastures on the river before they got caught in a snow storm.

We wintered on the river because it provided good protection from snow and wind, and also because it was closer to headquarters and easier to reach in bad weather.

So one afternoon I put together a small crew, consisting of me, Hobart Hall, Pat Mason, and Jake Parker. We trailered our horses six miles north of the river to the Smith place, gathered the cattle, and started them south through Leland Barby's country.

I had decided to run dry cows in the bridge pasture, so when we got there, we threw the herd in a corner and I cut out 16 dries. Pat and I drove them over a hill to water, and Jake and Hobart moved on south with the rest of the herd.

Most of the cows left in the herd had small calves, and they belonged in the middle meadow pasture. But there were two pairs with bigger calves and I wanted to take them to the west meadow, two miles upriver near headquarters.

We cut out the two pairs, left the others in the middle meadow, and started west with the pairs. The sun was going down by then, and it appeared that we would make it back home around dark.

This part of the river was heavily wooded with cottonwoods, willows, tamaracks, and locusts, and it was not ideal country to be driving cattle through. And to make matters worse, these two pairs started acting silly when we drove them away from the bunch.

We had gone about half a mile when they split and ran. One pair went north into the cottonwoods, and the other pair headed for the brush down on the river. Jake and I went after the north pair, and Pat fell in behind the other. Hobart had gone on because his gimp leg was bothering him.

Pat Mason, off duty, with the youngest of his four children.

By this time it was getting cold and dark. Jake and I picked our way through the trees and around fallen limbs and stumps. We followed our pair up a steep bank and then watched them build a new gate in a four-wire fence.

We let them go and rode back down to the meadow to see if Pat had done any better than we had.

When we rode up to the north bank of the river, we started yelling and calling for Pat. There was no reply, and we began to worry. Pat had been riding a small dun mare, and if he had roped his cow out in the brush, he might have gotten himself into a storm.

And if he was hurt and unable to call for help, we would have a devil of a time finding him.

A big full moon was up by then, and it gave us just enough light to see where we were going. We crossed the river and rode into the tamaracks on the south side. Every now and then we stopped and called. Still no answer. The farther we rode, the more we worried. Pat had a wife and four kids at home.

We were out in the middle of the brush when we heard Pat's voice in the distance. We hit a trot and rode toward the sound. We reached a clearing and there he was.

The full moon seemed to be sitting on his shoulder, and I could see the glow of his cigarette. He had forefooted the cow and bedded her down, and his little dun mare was braced against the rope.

Pat was sitting easy in the saddle and didn't seem to have a care in the world, as though forefooting cows in the moonlight was something he did every day.

Stanley Barby and two of his friends.

Chapter 12

Stanley Barby

Toward the end of October, the roundup crew moved over to the Open A's country on the Cimarron watershed. One morning as we were driving a big herd seven miles from the river to Knowles, I found myself riding beside Stanley back on the drag.

I kind of enjoyed riding drag, even though it was a little dusty when the wind was in the wrong direction. On long drives, a guy could play with his rope and practice heeling the slow cows.

That's what Stanley and I were doing, and as we rode along, I took this opportunity to ask Stanley some questions about roping. He knew about as much about roping as any man I'd met. For him, roping wasn't just a hobby or a passing fancy. He had made a life-long study of it.

He told me that his grandfather Barby had disapproved of roping on the original ranch. He had considered it a tool of last resort, and as a result, the hands never had a chance to practice their roping.

Nor did they have access to trained roping horses. Times were hard back then, and ranch horses came out of government remount studs and mustang mares. "They were tough but wild and un-trained," Stanley said. "They weren't good athletes and roping off them was dangerous."

Roping on the old Barby ranch atrophied. When the cowboys *had* to rope something, they didn't know how to do the job. Often they ran an animal to death, which to Grandfather Barby was further proof that the rope was a cattle-killer.

Stanley said that when he was a boy in the late 1940s, roping was so rare on the ranch that he considered it a major event, and he would ride to the top of the nearest hill so that he could watch.

But that changed in the early 1960s when the old ranch was divided up among the heirs. When Stanley got his part, he set out to make it a roping outfit.

Why?

"I've always had a passion for roping, and I've always wanted to go back to the old ways. When I was a kid, I had a rope in my hands all the time and I roped every cat, dog, and chicken on the place. When I took over my part of the ranch, I made it a roping outfit."

It wasn't easy to build a roping tradition where none had existed before. Stanley had to start from scratch. Most of the cowboys on the river didn't know how to throw a rope, they didn't ride trained horses, and they didn't know how to handle and throw roped cattle.

The first time he heeled and dragged calves to the branding fire, it didn't go well. Neighbors and older ranchers drove past the branding pen and watched. They left shaking their heads and saying, "It won't work. Roping is too hard on cattle and it's too hard on the men."

Stanley was discouraged, but he didn't give up.

That winter, he made arrangements to study roping technique under one of the greatest ropers of all time, Toots Mansfield of Big Spring, Texas. Stanley said of his teacher, "Toots modernized calf roping technique and put speed into it. I had watched other ropers, but I learned more about calf roping from him than anyone else. Toots trained me."

After he mastered calf roping, which is a hard-and-fast event, Stanley moved on to team roping and learned to dally and handle a loose rope. On weekends he pulled his horse to roping contests, and he often won.

Jake Parker, who learned to rope when he worked on the Bar B, once said that in his prime, Stanley could have held his own against the best ropers in America, and that if he hadn't been tied to the ranch, he could have competed in the professional ranks.

But Stanley was tied to the ranch, and running the ranch was his first love. Instead of becoming a professional roper, he took his knowledge and experience back to the ranch, applied them to his cattle operation, and began the slow process of teaching cowboys how to use the rope.

He didn't pontificate. He taught by example. When the cowboys saw him at work, they imitated him and went to him for advice. His mere presence on the crew raised the standards for everyone.

Around Stanley, it was impossible for a cowboy to settle into a comfortable mediocrity. The old days when a man could 4-or 5-loop a calf and still call himself a cowboy were gone, because Stanley was there and he could do it with one loop.

Stanley Barby: a deadly heeler in the branding pen.

He brought many changes and new techniques to the river country. He threw out the old-time method of roping hard-and-fast and replaced it with the dally method. Of the two, the dally was harder to master, but he felt it was better, safer for the men, and easier on the cattle.

He regarded the rope as a legitimate tool of the working cowboy—not the tool of last resort or a toy to be played with. There was a time and a place to use the rope, and when the time came, he expected his cowboys to know how to use it. He wouldn't hire a man who couldn't handle the rope.

He used the rope as a management tool. He believed that cowboys who could use it were superior to all the modern contraptions that had been invented to replace them, such as squeeze chutes, working corrals, tranquilizer guns, and so forth.

He figured that a roping cowboy could handle just about any problem that came up in the pasture and take care of it on the spot, without having to drive an animal several miles to a set of pens.

He also recognized that there was an important human factor involved in roping, something that non-ropers may find hard to understand.

"There is something about roping that creates an interest in a man. It's like being creative with your hands. There's a skill to it. To rope well, a man has to train his horse and train himself. He takes pride in what he's doing. You can't put a dollar value on that, but I think a man who takes pride in his work is better—better for himself and better for the ranch."

The strong roping tradition I had found on the river could be traced back to Stanley, and it was no accident that the best ropers in our country had all worked for the Bar B.

Chapter 13

Winter

By the middle of November, we had finished the fall roundup season and all the cowboys up and down the river went back to their home ranches to prepare for winter. On the John Little ranch, we laid in a supply of protein feed and hay and waited for the snow to fly.

1978 hadn't been a good grass year and I started feeding protein the day after Thanksgiving. Every morning I would back my pickup up to the cakehouse door and load my sacks of feed on the back.

Then I would drive down to the west meadow, call the cattle, and string out the feed in metal troughs. From the west meadow, I would drive down the river to the middle meadow and feed that bunch, then drive on down to the bridge pasture and feed those cattle.

The weather stayed open through December. We had some cold blustery days but no snow. Feeding cake in open weather wasn't hard work, just a little tedious after a while.

Around Christmas, it appeared to me that we were getting short on grass and that we had some cows that weren't holding their shape. These were old cows that we should have culled in the fall but hadn't.

Sometimes your old cows appear to be doing well in the fall, but when cold weather comes they begin to fall apart. When they are thin going into January, you have problems. A thin cow can't tolerate cold snowy weather as well as one that is in good shape, and after a big storm, you might find several of them dead.

I was worried about our thin cows.

Mr. Little had hoped that we wouldn't have to start feeding hay until February, but I told him that I thought the cows needed hay right now. He went with me on a feed run and looked them over, and he agreed.

The day after Christmas, I broke into the hay stack.

Four or five days later, I caught the 12:30 weather report out of KGYN radio in Guymon, Oklahoma. They gave a complete five-state forecast for Texas, Oklahoma, Kansas, New Mexico, and Colorado, and though they weren't always right, they came as close as anyone.

That day they said that a cold winter storm was moving down out of the Dakotas and that it would hit the Oklahoma Panhandle before morning.

It was getting late in the season and we were overdue for some nasty weather. If this storm turned out to be a bear, we might lose some cattle. I had spotted eight or nine cows that were thin, and I decided I had better bring them up closer to the house where I could keep alfalfa hay in front of them all the time.

After lunch, I drove over to the Three Cross and found Jake and his nephew Bud Parker working around the corrals. I told Jake about my problem and he agreed that we had better try to gather up the thin cows.

Jake and Bud saddled their horses and I saddled Little John, and we rode down the river to the middle meadow pasture. It was a warm sunny afternoon and we found the herd grazing on a flat north of the river. We pushed them into a corner of the fence and I cut out four cows.

Instead of taking them back to the home corrals, we drove them east into the bridge pasture, and while Bud trailed them up the fence to the northwest corner, Jake and I rode east until we found the bridge pasture cows near the south windmill.

Little John was a chargy, hard-mouthed horse who liked to take the bit in his teeth and run. You had to ride him with a tight rein and keep pressure on the bit. As we rode along, he was prancing. He felt good and wanted to run. I had to keep him pulled back, and all at once one of the shanks on the bit broke off.

That was a fine mess. I couldn't repair it out in the pasture and I didn't have time to go back to the barn and braze it. The storm was moving in our direction and we had about two hours of daylight left.

I yelled at Jake and he came over to see what was wrong. We studied the broken bit. I suggested that I might put a piece of baling wire in Little John's mouth and use the wire as both bit and reins. Jake shook his head.

He used a tie-down on Buck, a loop of heavy-gauge wire that went around his nose and fastened, by means of a strap, to a ring in the front cinch. Jake took that loop, tied it into my headstall, and then tied my reins to it. That gave me a kind of sharecropper's hackamore that would put pressure on Little John's nose.

We didn't know if it would work or not, but it was the best we could improvise on short notice. If Little John wanted to cooperate, I might be able to keep him under control. If he wanted to run and act a fool, then I would probably get a tour of the bridge pasture at a high rate of speed.

We rode into the herd and spotted several thin cows. Since I was broke down, Jake had to do most of the work, while I held the herd. He cut out three cows and we drove them up to the north end, where Bud was holding the four head we had cut out of the middle meadow.

We put them through the gate and drove them through pasture #6 for a mile and a half, then into the horse pasture and down to a hay feeder near the river. I had already filled it with good, bright alfalfa hay.

We had finished just in time. The sun slipped over the horizon and darkness began to fall. I thanked Bud and Jake, and we rode off in different directions.

It was a beautiful evening. A soft blue haze hung over the valley. Deer had come out onto the meadow to graze, and in the silence I could hear the calls of wild turkey, peacocks, and quail.

The next morning, fifteen hours later, the temperature stood at ten degrees and snow was falling sideways in front of a bitter north wind. At noon on New Year's eve, the temperature was five degrees and the chill factor had dropped to 35 below zero.

This was the beginning of a cold spell that lasted three weeks. The cows we had brought up to the horse pasture hardly moved away from the hay feeder, and I kept them well supplied with alfalfa. They all survived and we sold them in February, when the roads into Beaver dried up. Had we not brought them in when we did, I imagine that most of them would have died.

January was a hard month for all the cowboys on the river. In December, before the cold weather hit, I had fed the cattle six days a week, leaving myself a day off on Sunday. But after the first of the year, I started feeding seven days a week.

The boss didn't tell me to do this. The cattle did. They needed the extra groceries to get through the bitter weather.

It seemed that winter storms were stacked up all the way to the North Pole, and they hit us one right after another. We would have two days of snow, followed by a day or two of clear cold weather, then more snow, more wind, more temperatures below zero.

Through the month of January, I never took my pickup out of four-wheel drive. I never did get stuck in the pasture, but that was because I chose my route carefully and stayed away from deep snow drifts.

The days and weeks began to run together. One day was the same as the next and there was no difference between a Sunday and a Wednesday. I never saw anyone but my family and the Littles, and I never got off the ranch.

I went through the same routine every day. It began in the morning when I pulled on five or six layers of clothes and ended at night when I went to the house and started pulling them off. In between, I loaded sacks of cake and bales of hay and plowed through snowdrifts on my feed run.

In the afternoon, I went back to the hay stack and loaded up again. I had to feed the horses, the thin cows and the bulls in the corral, and fill the calf feeder in the west meadow pasture. Every animal on the place was cold and hungry and depended on me for feed. There were days when I felt sick, and there were other days when my back hurt and I could hardly stand the thought of lifting another bale of hay. But I had to make my feed run, no matter how bad I felt.

One morning I awoke before dawn and heard a strong north wind roaring in the tops of the cottonwood trees around our house. I got out of bed and discovered that the electricity had gone out. And it was snowing.

Our heating system went out with the electricity, so I turned on two burners on our propane kitchen stove and went back to bed. At daylight, the temperature was three degrees. The snow had stopped, but the high winds continued to blow, creating a phenomenon known as a ground blizzard: snow filled the air and drifted, even though it wasn't falling from the sky.

This was a brutal storm. The wind numbed your face and took your breath away and blinded you with swirling snow. You found yourself staggering through drifts and gasping for breath, and after walking fifty yards, you felt as though you had run a quarter mile.

I didn't make my feed run that day. It would have been useless. The cattle had drifted into the dense brush and the deepest holes along the river, and I couldn't have called them out to feed.

And it would have been dangerous for me to go out into the pasture. This was killing cold, the kind that could freeze a man to death. If I had gotten stuck in the pasture, or if the pickup had quit on me, I would have been in a bad spot.

Around nine o'clock, I walked up to the Littles' house and checked on them. The power was still out and, since the Littles' house had no gas appliances, they had lost their heat and were walking around in coats.

Mr. Little said that I had better start up the emergency power plant, a system he had installed a few years earlier for this kind of problem. The generator was powered by a four cylinder gasoline motor and it was kept in a tin shed north of the big house. It would generate enough electricity to run the heater fans in both houses, and maybe a few lights as well.

I trudged up the hill to the shed and looked over the generator, which hadn't been used in several years. With a screwdriver, I cleaned away the mud dobber nests around the flywheel and checked the gas.

Of course it was out of gas. I trudged back down the hill, filled a five gallon can with gas, and returned to the shed.

I was ready to start the motor. I hit the starter button and the motor turned over — once. The battery was dead.

I drove the pickup to the door of the shed and hooked up jumper cables to the batteries. Now I was ready. I hit the starter and the motor chugged, coughed, and started.

Black exhaust smoke poured out of the motor and filled the shed. It burned my eyes and I could hardly breathe. I was no mechanical genius, but it appeared me me that the gas mixture was a little rich. The motor was flooding out.

It ran for a minute or two, coughing and wheezing and popping, and then expired.

I walked down to the big house and reported this to the boss. He said that the float valve in the carburetor was stuck, and he gave me instructions on how to take it off. John Little was a pretty good shade-tree mechanic and could usually diagnose a problem in a pump or small motor.

I went back to the shed, removed my warm gloves, and, at three degrees above zero, began tinkering with this hateful little motor. I gutted the thing and took the carburetor down to the big house.

Mr. Little spread out a recent issue of the *Daily Oklahoman* on the kitchen table, set the carburetor on the paper, and went to work. Half an hour later, he had it fixed and put back together.

Dirt or something had caused the float valve to stick, he said.

Back at the shed, I put the motor together and fired it up, and this time it ran smoothly. We were in business.

Before I threw the switch and put electricity into the line, I had to go down to my house and unplug all nonessential appliances, such as deep freezes and refrigerators. Mr. Little did the same in his house, and shortly before noon, we were ready.

I walked back down to the big house and we went over our check list to be sure that we had followed all the procedures. It appeared that we had. Now all I had to do was throw two main switches at the power pole and plug the generator into the line.

I returned to the shed. The motor was humming along. I threw the switches and plugged in.

A moment later, my wife ran out of our trailer house and yelled, "Turn it off! Turn it off!"

Our emergency power system had just blown an electric clock off the kitchen wall and exploded a light bulb.

"Surge of current," Mr. Little said when I gave my report. "We must have a short somewhere."

I killed the engine and closed up the shed. That was all the good we got out of the emergency power system that winter.

Chapter 14

Winter Fun

Toward the end of January, everyone in my family had cabin fever. We had hardly been off the ranch since Christmas, and confined as we were in a small mobile home, we were getting on each other's nerves.

The two refrains most often heard around our house during this period were, "Ashley, stop playing in the toilet!" And, "Scottie, go to your room!"

One Saturday night, Kris and I decided that we had been cooped up long enough. We called up Sandy and Geneva Hagar, friends of ours who lived on the YL Ranch twelve miles away, and told them we were coming over for a visit.

The ground was still covered with snow, but Sandy said the roads into the YL were clear. We loaded the kids into our old Ford Pinto and off we went to the Hagars' for a wild night of making popcorn and drinking hot chocolate.

The night was clear and cold, around five degrees above zero. We didn't anticipate any trouble on the way, but any time we traveled through this isolated country in the winter, we dressed warmly and carried blankets in the car.

We drove seven miles north on dirt roads and didn't have any trouble. There were a few patches of snow and ice, but I had good mud grip tires on the Pinto and we went through them.

Then we came to a place where the road was lower than the pasture around it. It was always a bad spot. During rainy spells, it became a muddy swamp, and in snowy weather it drifted over.

I had gone through this cut in my pickup the day before and it hadn't been bad. I threw the Pinto into second gear and hit it with a full head of steam.

As soon as we hit it, I knew the snow had drifted during the day and it was too deep for the Pinto, but there was nothing to do but stomp on the gas and hope for the best. We got out in the middle of it and came to a stop.

I carried a shovel in the car, and I spent half an hour trying to dig and push us out. But it was hopeless. We were buried.

That seven mile stretch of road we had just driven didn't have one house on it, but we were fortunate that Paul Barby and his wife lived only a mile to the north, up on the flats. We wrapped the children in blankets. Kris carried Ashley, who was eleven months old, and I hoisted Scottie, age four, onto my shoulders. And off we went.

The air was clean and crisp. Huge silver stars twinkled in the black sky above us, and in the distance we could see the lights of towns in Texas, Oklahoma, and Kansas. It was a beautiful night for a stroll, except that we had to plod through snow, were carrying children, and the air was so cold that our breath froze on our chins.

Mr. and Mrs. Barby were watching television in their living-room when we knocked on the door. I hated to tell Fred what had happened. He was a cattleman and had been going through the same daily grind as I, fighting snow drifts and chopping ice and lifting bales of hay to keep the cattle alive.

Here he was, enjoying a quiet evening in a warm house, and we had come to disturb his solitude because I had miscalculated the depth of a snow drift.

We went into the house, pulled off our coats, and warmed our hands and feet. The first order of business was to get a message to Sandy and Geneva that we were safe. In ranch country in the winter, we all had to look out for each other. When someone didn't show up within a reasonable length of time, the whole neighbor-hood went on the alert.

I knew that if we didn't get a message out pretty soon, Sandy would call the Littles and they would all go out in four-wheel drive vehicles to look for us.

We called the Littles (it was our good fortune that the phones were working that night, which wasn't always the case), and they called Sandy and Geneva and told them what had happened.

We visited the Barbys for an hour or so, then Fred, Scottie, and I pulled on our clothes and went out to start the tractor. It was a big John Deere with a cab, dual rear wheels, and a snow blade on the front end. Fred had hooked it up to an electric engine warmer so that it would start in cold weather.

We fired it up, crowded into the cab, and drove south toward the Pinto.

This was all very exciting to Scottie, who had never ridden in a big tractor before. I doubted that Fred Barby found it very exciting,

Checking the weaning heifers in the corral.

but he was nice about it and let Scottie sit in his lap and hold the steering wheel.

Fred dragged the Pinto through the drift and then went back and plowed a path so that traffic could pass down the road. At ten o'clock we finally made it back to our house and told the Littles that we had arrived safely.

It had turned out to be an exciting Saturday night, though not exactly what we had planned. But at least we had gotten out of the house and had seen a couple of new faces. Now we were ready to stay home for the rest of the winter.

I reached the low point of the winter one day in early February. I had been working seven days a week for more than a month. I was physically tired from wading snow and mud, chopping ice, and lifting bales of hay, and I was emotionally tired from the strain of facing hungry animals and going through the same routine day after day.

That morning, I loaded up with hay and noticed that the new elk hide gloves Kris had given me for Christmas were full of holes. One month of handling hay had reduced my fifteen-dollar elk hides to rags! Then, half an hour later, I snagged one of my overshoes on some barbed wire and ripped out a hole the size of a half-dollar.

In my line of work, a man needed good gloves and a pair of overshoes that would keep his feet dry. I didn't have either one now. I didn't have the money to replace them, and I couldn't have gotten off the ranch to go shopping anyway.

But there were some lighter moments that winter. I remember one day in particular. It was a bitter cold Sunday morning in January. It had snowed for two or three days and the wind had whipped the snow into deep drifts. The storm had broken in the night and now the morning sun sparkled on the covering of fresh snow.

At 8:30 I drove my pickup down to the cakehouse and was about to step out when I heard a voice come on the two-way radio: "Unit 3 to unit 7, come in John."

I was unit 7. I keyed the mike and told unit 3, Stanley Barby, to go ahead.

Stanley came back on and said that he and Rodney had buried their four-wheel drive in deep snow, and he wondered if I could come over and pull them out. He gave me his location in pasture #5 on the Three Cross, and I told him I was on my way.

Then I called the Littles' base station and told them where I was going. They had been listening to the conversation and told me to

John and Scot dressed for the daily feed run.

Scot steers the moving pickup, while the old man breaks the bales and throws them out on the feed ground.

keep them informed. I signed off and headed for pasture 5.

I chuckled all the way because I knew how it must have galled Stanley to call for help on the radio. When a cowboy gets himself in a jam, he'd just as soon keep it quiet. But any time you talked on the radio, you could assume that your conversation would be heard by everyone along the river.

We had ten mobile units and three base stations on the network, and all of us listened to conversations on the radio. It was one way we had of keeping in touch with the neighbors and finding out what was going on. And in bad weather, we all tended to pay closer attention to the radio traffic. We learned where the roads were drifted over, and we didn't want to miss a distress call in case someone got in trouble.

That morning, when all the ranchers and cowboys were out breaking the roads and trying to get feed to the cattle, everyone along the river had his radio turned up and knew that Stanley had gotten stuck.

He had driven his pickup into one of those cuts in the road where snow had drifted several feet deep. You couldn't gauge the depth of the snow until it was already too late.

We hooked a nylon tow rope to his back bumper and I jerked him out. He thanked me, and he and Rodney went on their way, with their cowdog in the back of the pickup.

They were not yet out of sight when I got on the radio.

"Unit 7 to KTH 278, come in Mr. Little. I thought I'd better report back to you. I got Stanley unstuck and I'm on my way home. He'd found the only snow drift in the whole pasture and ran right into the middle of it. I told him that your hired hand doesn't have time to run a wrecker service, and that if he couldn't drive in snow any better than that, he ought to ride in the back with the dog and let Rodney drive. Unit 7 clear."

I waited for Stanley to come back, but the radio was silent. We both knew that up and down the river, all his friends and relatives were laughing beside their radios: Pat and Glenn and Junetta and Debbie, Lloyd and Ruth, Read and Jerry Lynn, Guy and Jan, Aunt May and Uncle John, Hobart and Kary and Darrell.

Stanley didn't forget that. The following spring he and his crew were helping me with some cow work in the bridge pasture. We finished the job before noon and started up the river in our pickups and trailers.

Stanley and his boys took the lead and I followed behind them. The meadows were boggy from spring rains and I hit a muddy spot.

I didn't have up enough speed, my trailer high-centered, and I was stuck.

Stanley stopped and came walking back toward me.

"What's the trouble?"

"I'm stuck."

He pushed his cap to the back of his head and flashed a big grin. "Stuck, huh? Well, if you want me to pull you out, get on the radio and call for help."

I gave him a wounded look, hoping to appeal to his better side. Nothing doing. He walked back to his pickup and I reached for the mike.

"Unit 7 to unit 3, come in, Stanley."

"Yeah, go ahead."

"Stanley, I'm stuck. Will you pull me out?"

"Is this *John Erickson?*"

"Ten-four."

"And you're *what?*"

"STUCK."

"Well, we ain't running a wrecker service, John, but I guess . . ."

Chapter 15

Leland Gets Hitched

Leland Barby was the owner of the Three Cross Ranch and lived about a mile upriver from us. At the age of 40, he was Beaver County's most eligible bachelor.

He was handsome and intelligent and a snappy dresser who bought good clothes and looked good in them. He had a pair of soft brown eyes and an easy-going smile. I always enjoyed working with Leland because he was a joker and, like me, he usually had some kind of mischief on his mind.

Right after the first of the year, he made a trip to Oklahoma City and stayed gone for a week. When he returned, he was a married man. He had married a girl named Sue, his old high school sweetheart.

This became the major news story of the winter in our little community, and everyone was happy about it. The older generation, which didn't quite approve of bachelorhood, heaved a sigh of relief, and all the aunts and uncles laid aside their lists of nice-girls-for-Leland.

There was also some hope that, now he was a married man, he might stop driving his Lincoln sixty miles an hour down ranch roads, while looking at grass, cattle, and clouds.

We cowboys rejoiced over Leland's marriage for a different reason. We hoped that his wife might be a good cook and that she would prepare meals when the roundup crew was working on the Three Cross.

Cowboys love a good feed. They think about it all morning and they talk about it all afternoon. Jo Ann Cox on the Open A and Junetta Barby on the Bar B prepared spectacular meals for the cowboys, and if a man walked away from their tables hungry, it was his own fault.

They were respected for their meat and potatoes, loved for their pies, cakes, and cobblers.

But during Leland's bachelor days, when a crew of men went to the Three Cross, they never knew what to expect at dinnertime. Jake

Parker told about the time the crew worked all morning, past noon, and into the afternoon. They kept checking their watches and wondering what had happened to the grub. Their stomachs growled and they became shaky with hunger, but they suffered in silence. Then, around two o'clock, Leland said, "Well boys, let's go to the house and see if we can scare up some grub."

The cowboys thanked the Lord and went to Leland's bachelor kitchen. "I don't know what we've got," he said, "but you boys just help yourselves."

Someone broke into the refrigerator and came out with four pieces of American cheese and eight or ten slices of stale bread. No mayonnaise, no pickles, no relish. The men divided up the bread and cheese and ate their dry sandwiches.

When they were done, one of them said, "I don't think I could hold another bite." Which became a famous line down on the river.

Far from being ashamed of this, Leland thought it was funny, and every time the story was told—and it was told every time a cowboy crew moved onto the Three Cross—he cackled with wicked laughter.

This happened only once to Jake Parker, who had been in the cowboy business long enough to take care of himself. From that day on, when he went to work on the ranch, he carried a lunch box full of food.

I missed out on the famous cheese sandwich episode, but I was present at another of Leland's feasts in the fall of 1978.

Stanley, Jake, Pat Mason, Glen Raven, and I helped Leland gather cattle out of pasture #3. Along about noontime, Jake began to hint that our belly buttons were rubbing on our backbones. He had brought his grub box, as usual, but he was worried about the rest of us.

Leland hadn't made any plans for lunch, so he suggested we drive up to the little hamlet of Knowles and get a hot sandwich at Jones' Store, a little grocery store that had frozen sandwiches and a new microwave oven.

So we climbed into Leland's Lincoln and had a terrifying drive to Knowles. When I finally got my ham and cheese sandwich, the outside was burned to a cinder and the inside was still frozen. I raised a howl about this, but the more I complained, the harder Leland laughed.

For dessert, he served each of us a Twinkie and a piece of bubble gum.

Well, Leland and Sue moved into the house on the ranch during

Leland Barby, the dapper owner of the Three Cross Ranch.

the cold spell in January. Since they had gotten married in a private ceremony in Oklahoma City, they decided to throw a big supper in Beaver so that all Leland's friends and relatives could get acquainted with his bride.

They reserved the community room at the Bank of Beaver City and set the date for February 3. Leland's aunts and lady-cousins got on the phone and invited everyone and told the wives to bring a covered dish.

And anyone who wished could bring a gift.

Kris and I didn't know what to do about the gift. We were broke. Doc Calhoon was still sending us duns for Scottie's last ear infection and I still needed a pair of overshoes. We just couldn't afford to be generous at that time, yet we didn't want to go to the shower with nothing.

So we decided to take a gag gift. I knew Leland would enjoy that as much as anything. We thought about it and came up with an idea. I found an empty vodka bottle and filled it with water. Kris wrapped it up in pretty paper and tied it with ribbons and bows. Then she wrote out the card in a neat feminine hand.

Dear Sue:
  Now that you are living with Leland, you might need this. We would be glad to come over some afternoon and show you how to use it.
                    Love,

              Aunt May and Aunt Gladys

Aunt May was May Little, my boss's wife, and Aunt Gladys was Gladys Howe who lived on the south side of the river. They were daughters of the Old Gentleman, and the sweetest, most grandmotherly ladies you ever wanted to meet. Both were active in church and Eastern Star, and the very notion that they might know what to do with a bottle of vodka was heresy.

The evening of the party, we scrubbed and preened and put on our best clothes, loaded the kids and the food and the gift into the Pinto, and headed for Beaver City.

The community room was already filled with people when we arrived. Children were darting here and there, playing games and having a big time. The ladies were back in the kitchen laying the feast out on long tables and getting everything ready.

There must have been somewhere between 80 and 100 people

in the hall, and most of them were Barbys, Barby in-laws, and Barby cowboys. It was quite a gathering of the clan. I hadn't seen so many Barbys in one place since the prairie fire.

Many of my cowboy chums were there, and when I saw them in their good clothes, I could hardly keep from laughing. I had never seen them wearing anything but jeans and chaps and cowboy hats. In their Sunday garb, they looked odd, like a bunch of steers that had just been dehorned and run through a dipping vat.

After the prayer, we lined up and filed past tables that were loaded down with food. This was an old-fashioned pot luck supper and the women had brought enough food to founder an army.

We filled our plates and the cowboy crowd drifted to the backside of the hall. I went that way and sat down at a table with Stanley, Read, Guy Paine, Jake, Keith Cochran, and Roger Chockley.

We minded our manners and discussed such solemn subjects as the depth of mud in Beaver County. This happened to be the subject closest to our hearts, since most of us had been walking and driving through mud for the last two months.

By the time we'd finished eating, someone at the front table was tapping a water glass with a knife and asking for quiet. Leland stood up and made a little speech, expressing his and Sue's appreciation for the shower and the gifts.

It was one of the funniest speeches I ever heard, because that was one of the few times I ever heard Leland Barby say anything that made any sense—and the only time I'd ever seen him trying to be serious.

Finally Leland shut up and sat down, and Sue stood up at the head table and began opening the wedding gifts. Two children brought her the presents. She opened one and held it up for everyone to see, and then she handed it to Jan Paine who held it up again and read off the name of the giver.

These were nice gifts: china and crystal and towels and things that Sue could use to set up housekeeping. Everyone in the hall was watching, and each gift touched off a little swirl of, "Oh, how nice," and "She can use that."

I thought of the vodka bottle and started sweating.

I had supposed that Sue and Leland would take the presents home and open them in private. Our little prank hadn't been intended for *the whole Barby clan*. The Barbys could be rather stern folk, and I knew that for three generations they had been solidly on the side of temperance.

They were not drinking people. They weren't even tasters.

Kris was sitting on the other side of the hall. Our eyes met. We were thinking the same thing: "This is going to be a disaster if we don't get it stopped."

Aunt May and Aunt Gladys would be insulted. The rest of the clan would be angry. Leland would laugh like hell when he got home, but here in public, in front of his aunts and uncles, he would have to pretend outrage.

My face burned and sweat popped out all over my head. The Barbys were good decent people and I didn't want to insult them.

Or lose my job.

Sue was working her way through the gifts, and she was getting closer to our little bomb. I could see it on the table. I considered sneaking around and taking it away.

No, that wouldn't work, not with a hundred people watching.

I thought of sending little Scottie up to steal it away, but no, that wouldn't work either. The boy had spent so much time around Jake and Leland and Lloyd that he couldn't be trusted with a serious mission.

The little girl who was ferrying the gifts picked up our present and handed it to Sue. My heart was jumping around in my chest like a jackrabbit in a gunny sack. I sank down in my chair, covered my face with a hand, and peeked through my fingers.

Sue wore a radiant smile as she tore off the paper. She held the bottle up and the smile froze on her lips. She read the card to herself and her face turned deep red.

This was her first appearance in front of the family and she didn't know how to handle this. Had she found a dead snake inside the wrapping paper, she wouldn't have been more shocked.

She said nothing, but handed the bottle to Jan Paine and went on to the next gift, her smile in shambles.

Jan glanced at the card and hurried out of the room. She ran back to the kitchen where her mother, Ruth Barby, was washing up the dishes.

"Mother! Look at this. *Aunt May and Aunt Gladys gave Sue a bottle of vodka!*"

Ruth was a wise woman. She had spent most of her life on the Beaver River and she could recognize a cowboy prank the minute she saw it. She assured her daughter that Aunt May and Aunt Gladys *had not* given liquor to the bride and that this was the work of some cowboy-devil.

Read Barby, bull rider.

Jan burst out laughing and brought the bottle back into the hall.

I saw her come back in. Peeking out between my fingers, I watched her go straight to her father. That was good. If there was anyone in the room who could appreciate the joke, it was Lloyd.

He read the card and squalled. He handed the bottle to Stanley, who read the card, looked straight at me, and shook his head, as if to say, "I know you did it because nobody in my family is that crazy."

The bottle and card went from hand to hand, all around the hall, and at every stop it brought an eruption of laughter. The one exception to this came when Lloyd carried it over to Aunt May Little.

She read the card and smiled, and said something like, "Yes, that's clever, isn't it?"

Our prank turned out to be the hit of the evening and, much to my relief, the Barbys weren't offended.

But I never could figure out how Mr. and Mrs. Little took the joke. For months the subject was never mentioned, and I took this to mean that since the rest of the family had enjoyed the prank so much, Aunt May and Uncle John had decided not to terminate me.

But then one day in the summer, the three of us were sitting around in their living room, talking about this and that, and the matter of the vodka bottle came up.

Aunt May's eyes sparkled and she said, "Yes, we thought that was very funny."

Maybe so, but they'd done a first class job of keeping it a secret.

Chapter 16

A Couple of Wrecks

Around the middle of March, Leland called me and asked if I could help him gather some heifers off of wheat pasture and move them to another place. I told him I could, after I fed and did my chores.

He told me to meet the crew in a wheat field about two miles south of Beaver.

I fed all my pastures, put out hay for the horses and heifers, saddled old Star, hitched up the stock trailer, ate a quick lunch, and headed up the river toward Beaver.

By the time I got to the field, Leland, Jake, and Leland's cousin Ralph Hughes were already bringing one bunch of heifers up the road, and I unloaded my horse and helped them pen them in an old wooden corral.

When we had this bunch corralled, we rode west into another wheat field and started gathering. These were heifers that Leland and Jake had weaned in the fall, and they were wild and silly, as only yearling heifers can be. We spilled them several times before they finally found the gate into the corrals.

Our horses had gotten soft and out of shape during the winter, and we put a lather on all of them before we finished the job.

We had a hundred heifers in the pens and Leland wanted to load them into trailers and haul them fifteen miles east to a patch of wheat he was going to graze out. We had four stock trailers and we calculated that we could haul the heifers in two trips.

We loaded up and started out. I brought up the rear. We went two miles north, then turned east on a paved farm-to-market road. I was driving along at about 45 miles an hour when a red pickup passed me. The driver had his warning lights blinking and he motioned for me to pull off the road.

I pulled over and he came up to my window. "Say, you lost one back there."

"One *what?*"

"One of whatever it is you're hauling in that trailer."

"*A heifer?*"

Yep, that's what he meant. One of those crazy heifers had jumped out of my trailer. He had seen her hit the pavement at 45 miles an hour. She had gotten up and staggered into the ditch.

I thanked him and went on.

At the east place, we unloaded our stock and I told Jake and Leland the news. They decided that if the heifer was able to move, we should try to drive her into a field on our way back to get the second load. That would get her off the highway until we could come back later with horses.

We headed back toward Beaver and found the heifer standing in the ditch. She had lost some hair and seemed a little shaky on her feet, but otherwise she appeared to be sound and unbroken.

I was surprised. If someone had asked me what would happen to an animal that jumped out of trailer and hit the pavement at 45 miles an hour, I would have bet money that it would have killed her.

The heifer wasn't dead, but she was certainly in a bad humor. When we parked our rigs and got out, she threw her head up and started pawing the ground.

We worked out a plan. Jake and Ralph got behind her and started her east down the fence. I went down the road a piece and opened a gate into a wheat field. When she came down the highway, I would stand in front of her and haze her through the gate.

Well, here she came, trotting down the fenceline toward me, and I yelled to let her know I was there. When she saw me, she shook her head, snorted, threw up her tail, and came straight after me.

I was standing in the middle of the highway, with no protection, nothing to hide behind. I jerked off my leather vest and prepared to use it in self-defense. But it fell from my fingers. I made a quick calculation and decided that if I stopped to pick it up, the heifer would get me.

There was nothing left for me to do but run.

Out of the corner of my eye, I saw a highway sign on the side of the road. To reach it, I would have to run toward the heifer, but I thought I could make it.

I made a dash for the sign, yelling and waving my arms.

If I had run away from her, I bet she would have chased me down, but when I ran toward her, she lost her nerve. All at once she turned south and jumped the fence into the field.

She never did see the gate I had opened for her, but that was all right. At least we had her off the highway.

We hauled the rest of the heifers to the east place, then went back for our horses. Leland had to go to some meeting that night, so

Donuts of hair on a fence between the ranch and Beaver.

he went on. Jake, Ralph, and I loaded our horses and drove our rigs back to the field where we had left the heifer.

The sun was setting by the time we got ahorseback, and we set out to find her. We would have to work fast.

We found her with a small bunch of cows. We eased her out and started her east toward the trailers. We all had our ropes down and Jake said that I could take the first shot. That was a kind gesture on his part, since we all knew that he was the best roper.

I spurred old Star into a run and off we went.

You'd think that after a heifer had fallen out of a moving trailer, she might have lost a little speed. But this old gal was a running Jesse, and Star, who had gotten fat over the winter, just couldn't catch her.

Jake and Ralph were right behind me, and I told Jake to take the shot, but by that time we had run out of field. The heifer went straight to the south fence, plowed through it, and kept on running.

We paused to make medicine. Jake and Ralph would go through the gate and follow the heifer and try to get a rope on her, and I would go back for a trailer and meet them somewhere in the next pasture.

By this time the sun had set and it was getting dark. I felt bad about the way things had turned out. Jake had given me first shot and I hadn't done my job. He said not to worry about it. All I needed was a faster horse or a longer rope.

I went back for the trailer and drove south into the pasture where the heifer had gone. I could see Jake and Ralph on the other side of a big draw. Jake was moving in for a shot. He kicked Buck into a run, stood up in the stirrups, and started swinging his twine.

Just as he was ready to throw, Buck stepped into a hole and lost his front legs. Jake rode him all the way to the ground, then at the last second, kicked out of the stirrups and hit the ground rolling.

Ralph was right behind him when the wreck occurred and came very close to running over the top of him. Buck did a flip and landed on his back. If Jake hadn't had good reflexes and known when to quit his horse, he might have been crushed under twelve hundred pounds.

As Ralph flew past Jake, he yelled, "You all right?" When Jake said yes, Ralph went on and roped the heifer before she could jump another fence. He was riding a young horse that he had never roped on before, and he wasn't too anxious to do this. But it had to be done, and he did it.

By the time we got the heifer loaded in the trailer, the moon was up and the stars were sparkling overhead.

At nine o'clock that night, I dumped the heifer out at the east place, forded the Beaver River south of Three Cross headquarters, and went home to a cold supper.

A couple of weeks later, I went over to Knowles to help the Open A gather cattle in several wheat fields. We sorted off 125 cow-calf pairs that Darrell Cox wanted to take north to the Cimarron country.

To do that, we had to drive the herd across Highway 64, just west of Knowles. We had done this several times before, and it had never been easy. It was a terrible place to cross cattle.

The old roadbed of the Katy Railroad ran right beside the highway. The Katy line had been abandoned several years before and the right-of-way had grown up in weeds. You never knew what you might find in there: rocks, wire, beer bottles, and half-buried railroad ties. Any time you rode into those weeds, you were taking a chance.

And of course there was the highway itself. Cattle don't like to cross a paved road. It's something they're not familiar with. When they come to the edge of a highway, they don't know what it is. Maybe it's water, maybe it's quicksand, maybe there's a booger out there just waiting to jump out and grab them. The surface is hard and slick and they have a hard time moving across it without slipping down.

Once we got them out on the highway, then we had traffic to worry about. Highway 64 was one of only two east-west highways that went through the Oklahoma Panhandle. It carried a lot of truck traffic, 'and when truckers went through that isolated stretch of country, they had the gas pedal to the floor and weren't looking for cattle or cowboys on the road.

If we'd ever lost a herd there, and if they'd run east, they would have gone right into Knowles, and we would have had to chase them through a little town that had barking dogs, lawnmowers, clotheslines, overgrown vacant lots, and other elements that can make cow work pretty difficult.

It was a lousy place to work, but the cattle had to go north. We had seven men on the crew that day—enough if everything worked right, but not nearly enough if we got into a storm.

We pushed the herd onto the apron of pavement in front of the highway. When they stepped on the black top, they began slipping around and getting nervous. Several calves ran through our line at the rear because our horses couldn't move fast enough on the pavement to head them.

Hobart Hall, Gene Hester, and I worked the drag and tried to ease the calves back into the bunch, while Pat Mason, Kary Cox, Randy Mason, and Rodney Barby held them on the east side and kept them from making a run through downtown Knowles.

Traffic from the east had come to a stop. A man in a cattle truck had seen what we were doing and had enough sense to stop and wait. Several cars were lined up behind him.

The road was clear to the west. This was our chance to make a safe crossing, but we couldn't get the lead cows to step out. We held them there for several minutes, cutting them off when they tried to run down the ditches and holding the calves at the rear.

Finally, the truck driver got impatient and drove past. The cars that had been stopped behind him went on too.

At last two or three cows crept out on the pavement and started across, and the rest of the herd followed—all but ten cows and calves that stayed on the south side.

One of these cows was partially blind, and she had made up her mind that she wasn't going to step out on that strange surface. I don't know why, but cattle often choose to follow the lead of a blind or half-blind animal, and that's what they did this time.

They tried to go east and we stopped them. They tried to go west and we stopped them. They circled and bawled, but they wouldn't go north.

We held them as long as we could, and then they started breaking away. It was inevitable. We couldn't move our horses fast enough to stop them.

When they broke, they went in several directions at once. The old blind cow headed west down the edge of the highway. Gene Hester was the closest man to her and he went after her. He was riding a nice little sorrel colt that he had just started breaking into cattle work. I was riding Little John, and I galloped west to back Gene up and keep the cow from cutting behind him.

All at once, I heard a loud crash behind me, followed by the sound of broken glass hitting the pavement and the scream of brakes. I threw a glance over my shoulder and saw a red car sliding down the middle of the highway, and a grown cow flying through the air.

The driver hadn't seen us and had crashed into a cow that had wandered out onto the middle of the highway.

I could see that the car was coming to a stop and that it wasn't going to plow into me and Hester, so I turned my attention to the cow we were chasing. If we didn't get her under control, she might cause another wreck that would get someone killed.

I was right behind Gene and yelled, "You'd better get a rope on her!" Over his shoulder, he shouted that he didn't want to rope a grown cow off his colt, for fear the colt would get jerked off his feet or dragged into the wire and junk along the roadbed.

Gene was a good hand and he showed good sense here. That was no place to train a colt.

I hollered, "Okay, turn her back this way and I'll take a shot."

Gene spurred the colt and rode hard, passed the cow, peeled her off the shoulder, and pointed her south into the weeds. I had a loop built and went in after her.

Little John stumbled over railroad ties and plowed through heavy weeds. I had never roped heavy stock off him before, and I didn't much want to now.

I still remembered what Pat Mason had told me: "When you get in a jam, that horse will quit you." But the cow had to be roped.

Little John staggered through the weeds and junk, gave me position, and I dropped my loop around her neck.

Several of the cowboys had jumped off their horses and run to check on the driver of the car, an older man from north-central Oklahoma. He wasn't hurt, though the car was badly damaged. Another cowboy had ridden east up the highway and was flagging down traffic.

Gene and I were worried about our position. If an eighteen-wheeler had come along at seventy miles an hour and swerved to miss the wreck, it would have wiped us out. We wanted to get to safer ground.

Gene got behind the cow and I turned Little John to pull and gave him some spurs. Maybe he'd figured out that this was the wrong time to loaf. He leaned into the rope and did his job.

As we were dragging the cow through the weeds, Hobart waved his arms and yelled, "Don't ride straight ahead! There's a bunch of hog wire in there." I hadn't seen the wire, and I was sure glad Hobart had. That could have led to disaster.

We finally got the cattle under control. A wrecker came out and towed the car into Beaver. The cow that had been hit was still alive on the side of the road, but so badly broken up that Kary got a .30-.30 out of his pickup and put her out of her misery.

Going down the road to the next roundup.

Chapter 17

A Sick Cowboy

We didn't get around to branding Leland's calves until June 5. That morning, eight of us gathered at the Three Cross, rounded up a pasture of cows and calves, and drove them into the pens.

We started the branding work around ten o'clock, and already we had ourselves a hot, still day. Rodney Barby and Randy Mason, Pat's boy, did the heeling and dragging. They were high school kids at that time, and both were good heelers. Jake, Pat, Bud Parker, and I took turns wrestling and doing the other chores, and Leland ran the branding iron.

Several years before, Leland had decided that an electric branding iron was an improvement over the standard equipment (irons heated in a propane fire), and he'd bought one. He was the only rancher on the river who used it. The electric iron stayed hot and made a pretty brand, but, obviously, you had to plug it into an electrical outlet, which wasn't always handy in a branding pen.

To solve that problem, he had rigged up a long electric cord that plugged into a socket near the loading chute and ran out into the arena where we were doing the work. The iron plugged into a metal electrical box that had three or four sockets in it.

It worked fine for the first hour, then one of the cowboys said he smelled smoke. Leland walked over to the plug box and looked at it. Then he did what any sensible cowboy-electrician would do when he must repair a piece of equipment he doesn't understand: he picked up the box and began poking, fiddling, and twisting wires in hopes that the problem would correct itself.

While he was doing this, we had a calf on the ground and were waiting for the brand. The work had come to a halt and we were all watching. Suddenly the box erupted in sparks and flames, and Leland's head disappeared in a cloud of white smoke.

He dropped the box, threw up his arms, and yelled, "Hyah! Hyah!" Once again, a cowboy had managed to salvage comedy out of the rubble of human experience.

By twelve o'clock, we were all hot, tired, dry, and hungry.

Leland had mentioned that his wife had gone to Oklahoma City that day, and several of us began to wonder about the grub situation—if we were going to get another of Leland's famous roundup dinners.

The noon hour came and went. The crew went on working but there was no joking among the boys and very little talk. We were all weak with hunger. At a quarter to one, Jake pointed out that we still had three hours' work to do and that maybe we should stop for lunch. Leland agreed and said that he would take us into Beaver for a good hot meal.

That brought smiles to our faces, and we loaded into Leland's pickup and headed for town. Leland, Jake, Pat, and I rode in the cab, and the boys rode in the back end.

We went to the Motel Restaurant and took a big table near the back. We must have been a pretty rough-looking bunch when we walked through the cafe. We still had our spurs on, we were dusty and sweaty and speckled with dehorning blood, and I imagine that we brought some of the fragrance of the branding pen with us.

We all ordered chicken fried steaks. When the lady brought Jake's and set it down in front of him, the cream gravy was still steaming hot, so he waved his hands over it and said, "Hyah, hyah!" That drew a big laugh, and Leland cackled louder than any of us.

After lunch, Randy and Bud took out their tins of Skoal and loaded up. Rodney didn't use tobacco very often, but this time he decided he would. He took a pinch out of Randy's can and put it under his lower lip.

We all piled into the pickup and headed east toward the Three Cross, thirty minutes' drive down the river.

We had just cleared the city limits when Bud stuck his head in the window. He was wearing an odd smile. "Rodney's got sick on that snuff. He thinks he might have to throw up."

We all looked back at Rodney, who was sitting very still and leaning back against the tail gate. His eyes were hollow and his face was the color of oatmeal.

Bud continued: "Do you want to pull over so he can . . ."

"Hell no!" said Leland. "Tell him to hang his chin over the tail gate and get after it. And tell him if he messes on my pickup, he has to clean it up!"

Bud delivered this message to Rodney, who tried to smile.

By the time we crossed the Clear Creek bridge, three miles east of town, poor Rodney was heaving over the side and everyone in the pickup was laughing. Now and then his head would appear, he

Bud Parker, with tin of snuff in his righthand shirt pocket.

would give us a weak grin, and then he would hang over the side again.

Twelve miles east of town, we crossed the river on a rickety old bridge known locally as Barby Bridge, and we passed within a mile of Rodney's home. Leland stuck his head out the window and yelled, "Hey, cousin, do you want me to swing by the house and let your momma see what you've been doing?"

Rodney's head was over the side at that moment, but he waved his arm in a manner that told us no, he didn't think Junetta would be very proud of him right now, thanks.

By the time we reached the ranch, Rodney had left a trail of chicken fried steak eighteen miles long. Some of the color had returned to his face and he was feeling better. Leland pulled up in front of the house, turned on the garden hose, and let Rodney run some cold water over his face.

He was a good sport about it, and after sitting in the grass for a few mintues, he began laughing with the rest of us.

Leland stood over him and shook his head. "Next time, I'll just feed you a cheese sandwich. No sense in wasting a good chicken fried steak on you. You'd just puke it up."

Epilogue:
November 13, 1984

I left Cowboy Country in August of 1979 and moved to Texas to take a job on the LZ Ranch south of Perryton. Though I worked on the river for only a year and a half, it was an important period in my life. I learned my trade under some good men, the best cowboys I've known. I'll always be grateful that I had the opportunity to ride with them.

Over the years I've tried to keep up with the folks on the river, but it's been hard. You get caught up in your own little world. Time slips away. People move on. Things are never the same. But I was in Beaver yesterday and had the chance to catch up on the news about my old cowboy friends.

Jake Parker is still working on the Three Cross for Leland. A horse went down with him last year and broke his ankle. He had to lie around the house for a while and just about drove Audrey crazy. He was so desperate for something to do, he even read some of my books. But it didn't take him long to figure out how to stay in the saddle with a cast on his leg. When I left the river in 1979, Jake was nursing a side of broken ribs from a similar wreck. He's keeping the doctors in business, old Jake.

Leland and Sue Barby are living in a new house on the Three Cross, and he still looks dapper and trim. Leland says he's now taking orders from three women: Sue and their two teenage daughters. He still owns the old green Lincoln that he used to drive sixty miles an hour down those rough roads. That Lincoln has probably put more cars into the ditch than any vehicle in Oklahoma.

Stanley and Junetta Barby are grandparents now, and Stanley has bought himself a two-passenger helicopter. When I first heard that, I couldn't believe it. I didn't think there was any way you could get Stanley Barby off a horse. But he's having fun with his flying machine and uses it to gather cattle out of the big brushy pastures along the river. Whether he's figured out how to rope out of the helicopter, I don't know, but I'll bet he's thought about it.

Rodney went two years to Clarendon Junior College in Clarendon, Texas, and was on the rodeo team. I hear he's become a fine roper. Now he's transferred over to Panhandle State in Goodwell, Oklahoma, where he's sharing an apartment with Bud Parker. Bud works in the meat department at Panhandle State. I wonder if Rodney has tried snuff since that day in 1979 when he lost his chicken fried steak.

Read and Jerry Lynn Barby are living in Goodwell and recently had their third child, a baby boy. Guy and Jan Paine are still living on the ranch and they just had their third child, another boy.

Lloyd and Ruth Barby sold their interest in the Beaver Livestock Auction, but they're still running rodeo stock on their place north of the river.

The Open A has changed a lot since I knew it. None of the cowboys I worked with—Aaron Miller, David Dunn, Hobart Hall, and Carl Githens—are there anymore. Darrell Cox has leased the ranch from the Ralph Barby Estate and takes in outside cattle. Kary Cox has his own place south of the river.

John and May Little are still on the old Barby headquarters place, where we used to live. I haven't seen them in a long time, and I hear that Mrs. Little's health is not good. They must be close to eighty now.

Pat Mason left the Bar B several years ago and moved his family up to Kansas. Seems to me I heard he's managing a ranch up there. Last I heard, Randy was going to school at Clarendon Junior College. He grew into a tall, fine looking young man.

Glenn Green moved off the Allen Place after the spring round-up of 1979 and lived in Higgins, Texas, for a while. The last news I got on Glenn was that he was working in a feedlot near Bushland, Texas.

And Hobart Hall? We buried him yesterday. That's what I was doing in Beaver, and that's how I happened to catch up on the news of all the cowboys. Most of them were there. Lloyd Barby was a casket bearer. Jerry Lynn and Read sang a duet, and Jan Paine played the organ.

Hobart stayed on the Open A until 1980, then he retired after serving twenty-seven years as a Barby cowboy. He and Minnie moved to Beaver, and he took a job working for the county. The next time I saw him, in the spring of 1981, he'd acquired something he'd never had before: a pot belly.

Hobart Hall, 1916–1984.

Naturally I gave him a hard time about it. I patted his belly and asked when he was due to foal, and made cracks about his prosperity showing. He bristled and fought back. It was just like old times.

It must have been about two years ago, in January of 1982, that Minnie got cancer and died. I didn't hear about it until after the funeral. I often wondered how old Hobie was doing, and through friends I heard, "Not so good."

I didn't know Minnie very well. She struck me as a big, quiet, strong country woman who fussed over Hobart and knew how to put up with all his growling and barking—the kind of good woman who sticks with a good man and makes him better.

Hobart didn't talk much about her. That wouldn't have been "cowboy," since everybody knows we're big and tough and don't need the soft loving touch of a woman. But I could tell, just by the way he spoke of "me and Minnie," that he was fond of her.

It's funny about big tough cowboys: how quickly they age and fall apart when their wives are gone, how small and lonely they look when they have to dress themselves and feed themselves and go home to an empty house at night.

I saw Hobart for the last time about a month ago. I went up to the Beaver County Fair and ran into him out by the snow cone stand. As usual, we exchanged news about our cowboy friends. Standing there with our hands in our pockets and with the wind blowing sand in our faces, we had a few laughs about the old times on the river.

Hobart knew that I was writing this book. I told him I'd finished the manuscript and that Kris had been developing the photographs in her darkroom. I said, "The other day, I walked into the darkroom and saw five pictures of you hanging on a wire to dry. It almost scared me to death." He liked that.

Then it was time to go, and I said, "Well, Hobie, I better get along. Take care of yourself and I'll see you at the rodeo next spring. We'll have our book by then."

He didn't say goodbye. He started crying. I didn't know what to say, so I turned and walked away. I looked back and he was still standing there. I think Hobart knew he would never see the book.

So yesterday I drove up to Beaver, expecting to attend a small service at the Christian Church. But it wasn't a small funeral. Even though I got there twenty minutes early, I had to park two blocks away. Hobart would have gotten a kick out of that, making me walk two blocks to his funeral.

Inside, the church was packed. That says a lot about Hobie. Even though he lived most of his life on isolated ranches and had little opportunity to get out and meet people, those who did know him were fond of him.

I had to stand in line to sign the guest book, then I paused beside the open casket. The man inside didn't look much like the Hobart I remembered. His face was thin and waxy, and they had put a little too much paint on his lips. But they had fixed his flat-top haircut right. He still looked like a porcupine.

A spray of blue carnations lay on the casket lid, with Hobart's cowboy hat on top of it—his town hat, not the old greasy thing he used to wear in the pasture. I'll bet Minnie sent that one to the trash when they moved to town.

After the service, I rode out to the Fairview Cemetery with Jake and Audrey Parker and Leland Barby. It was a bright fall afternoon with warm sunshine and no wind. The thirty-mile drive to the Clear Lake Community took us down the Beaver River valley, and it brought back many fond memories of Hobart and the time I spent in Cowboy Country.

I remembered a story Hobart told me about the cold winter day when he and another man had to cross the Beaver River to check some heifers on the other side. On their way back, they were wading stirrup-deep water when Hobart's horse went down in quicksand. He went over the horse's head, and before he could get away, the floundering horse struck him with a front foot, pushed him under the icy water, and *stood on him.*

Had his cowboy companion not come to his rescue, he would have drowned.

And I recalled another Hobart story. One day, many years ago, he drove some horses to Barby headquarters and was about to ride back to rejoin the cowboy crew, when he heard a lady's voice: "Oh Hobart, would you mind helping me with something?"

Hobart, being a proper cowboy gentleman, went up to the yard to see what Mrs. Otto Barby needed.

She was getting her flower beds ready for planting. She gave him a shovel and a wheelbarrow, and Hobart spent the next four hours shoveling barnyard manure, pushing it up the hill, and spreading it on her flowerbeds—in his chaps and spurs!

Twenty-five years after the incident, when Hobart told me the story, he was still fuming about it. "Hauling manure in a wheelbarrow!" he snarled. "That woman sure didn't understand cowboys. From then on, every time I saw her I ducked behind the barn and hid out!"

And I remembered something May Little had told me about Hobart. She said, "Oh, he's the sweetest, kindest man, and such a gentleman. One thing I've always admired about Hobart is that he doesn't curse and swear."

I just nodded and smiled. If Mrs. Little had heard Hobart tell the story about hauling manure for Mrs. Barby, she might have changed her mind about his cursing and swearing.

We buried Hobart beside Minnie in the little Fairview Cemetery, overlooking the Beaver River valley and the sand hills on the other side. I had ridden all that country with Hobart, and I knew I was going to miss the old rascal.

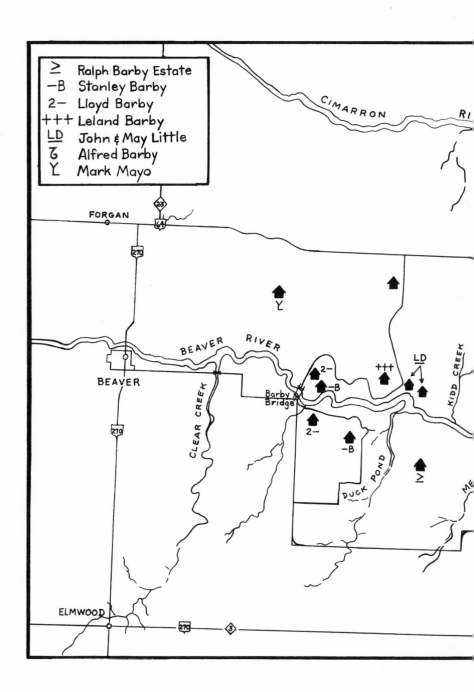